Sandlot Stories

Marcella Parsons: Coach
and
Steven Hayes Young: General Manager

ARose Books
Incline Village

Made in the United States of America

Copyright © 2003

ARose Books
Incline Village, NV

ISBN 0-9740636-7-3

Library Of Congress Control Number: 2003092332

The cover is a painting by local Lake Tahoe artist,

Theresa Lacey

entitled "I Could"

Cover design by _Katherine Parsons_

Table Of Contents

Table Of Contents

Table Of Contents

Table Of Contents

The Sandlot Game

This book, "Sandlot Stories" actually became like a Sandlot Game itself.

From across the world, the first two players came together from different cultures and languages to share their own sandlot stories with each other. Thanks to Atsuro for being the first player to come to the game and discuss childhood baseball stories with his good friend Steven Hayes Young. "Sandlot Stories really began when Atsuro asked Steve, "What was it like for you as a child playing baseball?"

Then Steve and I got into casual discussions about our childhood baseball experiences and together, the vision of capturing sandlot stories of youth came to us both. This took us through our amazing sandlot game in which we started with nothing more than an idea, the blank book—our sandlot. The next thing to do was to put down the bases and get the players!

Before the game even got started, Steve took on the role of General Manager (GM). With his background in business and baseball, he went out as our sandlot GM to seek the players. His relationships across the world provided friends with varied and interesting backgrounds. He brought each player to the sandlot game and encouraged them to share a story from the heart about their own childhood and baseball.

I took on the role of coach, blending each player's story

The Sandlot Game

and unique skill into the sandlot game. Looking back on the past, our players brought their childhood game, tinged with a pleasant glow like a summer evening sunset while playing ball—leaving behind a rosy afterglow of sandlot memories—capturing a place and a moment in time.

As people came to our sandlot, some had peanuts, hot dogs and watched; others came and left; others went home to think about it; and still others came to play. Everyone was welcome! Those who came to play, all came for the love of baseball, the love of the sandlot game!

With The Opening Pitch our sandlot game was started with childhood memories. As we approached the "Seventh Inning Stretch," the game progressed and we headed into the ninth wondering if we would win. But then in the final innings we realized in our hearts that like all good sandlot games, The Game Never Ends.

It is our hope that our fellow baseball fans will not only enjoy reading this, but be reminded of their moment in the sandlot of their youth. As for others, we hope you will enjoy the nostalgia of each individual experience described in these pages portrayed through the innocent eyes of youth with baseball as its backdrop.

—*Marcella B. Parsons*
Coach

The Next Generation Of Sandlot Sluggers

To my children, their friends, their teammates, with all their little sandlot fields, may they create a next generation of sandlot memories for you.

To my wife who keeps the sandlot game going for everyone by patching up the "*oweeeees*" and scrapes with bandaids, soothing the bumps from errant throws, and always stepping up to the plate for an occasional swing, much to everyone's delight.

To my brother, who amazes us each summer with his architectural and construction talents—with new additions for their sandlot. The first summer started with laying out a basic field and bases without obstructions from the pine trees. Next came designing a backstop from an old screen door; followed by uncovering a smooth infield hidden underneath mounds of pine needles. Who knows, the dreams for next summer continue with potential plans for a bleacher section made from the abundant supply of cut logs or even hanging a light in the trees for night games.

And thanks to our neighbors, watching the game over the fence, for sharing a memory or two of your own with us, and encouraging the homerun hits that end in your yard.

It's all about sandlot baseball . . .

— *Steve*

Dedicated to:

K. and D.

   Yesterday I hiked up to the top of the mountain to see the wildflowers in bloom and look at Lake Tahoe. On the way I was thinking about you both—your life growing up—and realized that it was just like a Sandlot Game.

   You probably thought as small children that your life would be like Little League with a mature coach to lead and guide you, cool uniforms, funding, a nice field, bleachers, and a team to be part of, giving a sense of belonging and security. But what you got was a kid only slightly older than you two who only knew a few rules of the game to pass on—those of safety and fair play. We often had to improvise for a bat or ball and often didn't even know where we would play the game. I know I was always on the search for a better sandlot across the country and back. Funding was unsure and we didn't have cool uniforms(those Catholic school ones don't count). Some innings were tough and some were down right hilarious, but you two kept stepping up to bat and swinging and for that I always admire you both.

   Now you are grown up and off onto new innings of life. I have no more words to express how proud I am of both of you—what a team!

— Mom

Opening Pitch

Kusa-Yakyu

I am pleased to talk about my Sandlot game because that is the one I used to enjoy playing a lot when I was young, and it was the best memory of being a child for me.

First of all, the term Sandlot game, *kusa-yakyu* in Japanese, is used widely, including the game played by kids or one played by an adult at a baseball field. The game is played by teams other than professional, school, or company owned teams and is called *kusa-yakyu.*

It was 1983 to 1988 (I was a little boy from ten to fifteen years old), when I played *kusa-yakyu.* The game was played at a small park, actually a field beside the bank of a river, or on vacant land near my house in Nagoya.

When I was a kid it was not difficult to find a place to play, but my home was not in the center of a city. It was more a kind of a suburban area. But now-a-days, the places to play *kusa-yakyu* are getting less and less, especially in big cities. I liked a Dragons' player at that time, which helped me to be interested in baseball. Ken Mocha from the U.S. was the Dragons' player I liked most.

It is common in Japan that a river- side bank has a baseball field. I think the reason why there was often a baseball field along a river-side bank is that in Japan there are few flat, vacant land areas in big cities. Only a park or the river-side would have it.

I remember that we dropped the ball into the river many

Sandlot Stories

times and had to catch it by net. We lost baseballs a lot not only in the river but also in the bushes as well.

We put gloves down or drew a square on the ground as bases. The number of players varied from six to twelve, but girls never played.

As children grow up and go to junior high school, they usually join a school club to play baseball. But I didn't. So I played *kusa-yakyu* with my school friends a lot, almost every day at that time, spending wonderful times with my friends. This is why I remember it so much.

In high school, I joined the soccer club at school. So I didn't play *kusa-yakyu* any more.

— *Atsuro*

• • •

As for my nickname, I was called just Atsuro or Atchan, which is not so funny though—"-chan" is a suffix in Japanese that is usually used when people call children or girls. My friends in Sandlot baseball had some cute nicknames. Yamaguchi was called "Gucci""Anju" for Ando, "Koba" for Kobayashi, "Okarin" for Okajima and so on.

• • •

My favorite baseball player's number was No.7 of Masaru Uno. He was a home run batter in Chunichi Dragons, my hometown baseball team.

My Sandlot

A Typical River-Side Sandlot

Baseball Began in the City Streets

The beginning of "sandlot" baseball for me was the dream of all young boys wanting to play the game. In the suburbs of New York City, town of Flushing, the contrast between then and now was like night and day. The night being the black top streets and the day, the green grass and gold fine fields our youth experience today. I learned the game from my older brothers and the neighborhood kids. Baseball began in the city streets, where home plate was a manhole cover, first and third base a mark on the curb and second a chalked square in the middle of the street or another manhole cover.

We began playing a game called "punch ball." The field was the same, the method of hitting was with our fist, so began our first lessen in eye to hand coordination. The game could be played with any number of players. When there were more than two, the teams were divided by "choosing up sides." We used an odd or even finger game called "Finns," where two players would put out one or two fingers on the count of three. If the count of both players' fingers was even, then the even man won the right to choose first; if the count of both players' fingers was odd, then the odd man chose first. Another method of determining teams was "tossing the bat." One of the two captains would be tossed the bat, catching it with one hand. Then alternating hands, the two captains would work their way up to the end of the

Sandlot Stories

bat, leaving the smallest amount of bat at the handle or knob for one player to grasp. The player left with the bat would hold it at arm's length, as the other player attempted to kick it out of his hand. Holding on to the bat gave that man the right to choose first. If he dropped the bat, first pick went to the other player.

From punch ball we graduated to "stickball." The name came from sawing off the broom of a broomstick and using the handle as a bat. The game received notoriety from Willie Mays, when he was pictured in the newspaper playing in the streets of New York. The pitching was either on a line or a bounce, so the pitcher could put "English" on the ball. "English" was spins put on the ball to have it go right or left, stop, or gain speed. The same rules as in baseball applied except when the trees, parked cars or a passing car delayed the game. Again, we divided the teams unless there were an odd number of players, then the youngest, usually me, was the token player. Thinking back, it made me a better player, because I had to prove to them I was good enough to be picked.

We played it in the same location as punch ball, but now the trees lining the streets came into play. The outfielders found it more challenging, as they had to judge long fly balls as they came off the bat and then reappeared out of the trees. I remember this "V" where the trees came together giving you a little window to judge the ball. We played almost every day and sometimes into the darkness, especially during the summers. Score was kept using chalk to mark a box score on the ground to keep track of the innings and score.

Sandlot Stories

There was a girl, Eileen, who lived in our building, a few years older then me. She was a "tomboy," a name given to a girl who played boy's games. She was a very good baseball player, and could hit, catch and run better than most of the boys. I remember one time playing stickball, when she hit the ball so far and hard, I couldn't believe it. She was pretty too, and as she got older, she played less and less. I think she figured it was better to do girl things. She moved away awhile later and we lost contact.

Another game was "strikeout". A rectangular box was marked on a wall with the chalk. The box was the strike zone of a batter—same size fit all. It was located on the wall between the candy store and the drug store. The pitcher threw from the rubber, a mark in the middle of the street, and could throw a fastball, curve, drop or whatever. The chalk had a double usage. If the batter let a pitch go by thinking it was a ball and it hit the line, we had the proof of the chalk on the ball that it was a strike. The foul line were points marked on the apartment building cross the street; a single was anything hit on the ground, a double the first floor, triple the second floor and home run was a cement decorative line above the second floor. We made an out by having a grounder or fly caught, or a strike out. Score was kept the same way as in stickball. The hazards remained with the parked cars and passing cars, but the trees were replaced by the windows of the apartment, which if hit, were an out.

And, oh yes, if someone broke a window, they had to go own up to the person whose window was broken. I remember breaking our dentist's window one day, running

Sandlot Stories

for cover, and then later knocking on his door to fess up to the damage and finding out he had had a patient in the chair at the time.

As I got older, I was able to go to P.S. 32, or the "school yard", two blocks away from the house. The field for strikeout was bigger, with the fence further back. The bar in the middle of the fence divided the double and triple and the home run was now over the fence. Over that home run fence was a regular sized field. It looked like black exposed aggregate. It was a normal size, either for softball or baseball, with painted lines and bases. We used the regular wooden bats and all the rules applied. There were no cars, traffic or trees to tend with now or get in the way. The new fear was challenging, and being challenged, to see who was the best at playing the game, at least for that day.

Sliding was a "cool" thing to do, except Mom didn't like it much, because we tore holes in our dungarees or got a big strawberry on our hip or thigh when we slid. This was fun, but when I told my children about it, their comment was, "Oh yeah, sure Dad" or they'd give me a look that said, "Who do you think you're kidding?" Kind of like the story, "and you walked to school ten miles in the pouring rain and snow."

P.S. 32 was open for summer school recreation and it was the place to go during the summer to do anything. There were contests in all the activities like shuffleboard, hockey (similar to air hockey), volleyball, and we could do crafts. We also played organized games of softball against the other summer schools.

8

Sandlot Stories

At the age of ten years plus, I had saved enough money from shoveling snow for the neighborhood butcher and a few other neighbors, to buy my own baseball glove. Until then, I had shared a glove, played barehanded or sneaked one of my brother's gloves, then having to get it back in before I got caught. The last one always got me in trouble.

I had heard of a new sports store by the name of Tony DePhillips Sport Shop. So, one night my father, "Pop" took me after work. I picked out this beauty of a mitt and met Mr. DePhillips. After buying the glove, he told us about a league he was forming, the "Tony DePhillips Athletic League." He was a backup catcher for the NY Yankees. I'm not sure, how long the league lasted, as the years went by I lost contact.

We began playing on the "Golden Estates" in Bayside. It was a beautiful estate with a large gate, gravel driveway, and beautiful rolling grass hills that seemed to go forever. The house was big and elegant and overlooked Little Neck Bay, off the Long Island Sound. Some of the fields were level and others were nestled in the hills. The fields were three miles from the house so we walked, rode the bike, or got a ride from the coach and sometimes from Pop. We had tryouts and were put on teams, got uniforms and even had a team picture with our sponsor, a nursery. A father who was a New York City police sergeant coached the team. It was a good team. We practiced a few times a week and played a couple of games each week. We finished the season doing pretty well. Once while I was pitching a game, I was throwing hard, but not too many strikes, and they started calling me "Windy".

Sandlot Stories

After a couple of years, Golden Estates was sold to build houses and the fields were moved. The new playing area was a real sandlot, leveled by graders and bulldozers, and just in time for the new season. Wooden backstops were constructed and the bases setup, but the field didn't get any professional work done to it. All the parents and kids walked for hours picking up rocks, so that grounders could be fielded without anyone getting hurt. No grass was seen for at least the first year. I moved on to another league by the time the grass came up.

I remember walking through a park one day, while we were still playing at the Golden Estates and seeing a really nice field with flags and a wooden fence in the outfield. Yep, it was the start of Little League. I remember looking in awe at the field, uniforms, etc. and thinking, you may look better but we can play better. I remember my friends and I trying to arrange a challenge game with a little league team, but that never happened. I moved on to play in other leagues and church leagues after that.

Pop took me to the Polo Grounds to watch Giants' games. We sat in the left field upper decks where I bugged him for hot dogs and candy. As I got older we moved to the lower deck behind first base. Two stories remain in my memory. One, the night a line drive foul was hit by Johnnie Mize straight at us. Pop stuck out his hands, caught the ball and then dropped it into the lap of a man sleeping in front of us. Pop wouldn't pick it up off his lap; the man woke up and kept the ball, even after people told him what had happened.

Another night, the Boston Braves were playing. As always,

Sandlot Stories

when we were there and Bobby Bragen was walking to the dugout before the game, Pop would stand up and yell, "Hey Bobby" and he would look up, smile, and wave to us.

One of the highlights of the Tony DePhillips League was the end of the season banquet. Trophies were given to the winning teams, MVP, best batter and best sport, and a picture was taken. Also, we met celebrities like Don Larson who later threw a perfect game for the Yankees, Bobby Bragen of the Boston Braves and a famous boxing referee. The night Bobby Bragen attended, we had a chance to sit and talk with him over drinks of soda. I kept on poking Pop to ask Bobby about when he came to town for the Giants' games. Bobby finally said, "What do you want to ask me?" So I asked him if he remembered someone calling out his name at the ball game. With a big grin he said, "Yeah, was that you?" He said he always looked forward, when coming to New York, to hear a friendly fan calling his name. Most places he visited the fans usually booed the opposing team and coaches.

I joined the church league, playing Sunday double headers, some at Golden Estates before the final sale of the property. I continued playing baseball in high school and two years at Windham College in Vermont. I moved to California, was cut by a university team, where five players were drafted to the majors two years later. My story continues into company softball leagues, coaching little league baseball and softball, and currently coaching high school softball. But those are other stories.

— *Bill Wright*

11

Sandlot Stories

Little Pirate

I was born outside of Pittsburgh, Pennsylvania in 1958 and grew up with the Pirates as my team. Pittsburgh is famous for many things including its baseball team, The Pirates, and its three rivers that converge at "The Point." The Allegheny and the Monongahela come together to form the mighty Ohio River that flows west from Pittsburgh to the state of its name. For many years the Pirates have played ball in Three River's Stadium across from The Point, but when I was young they played in Forbes Field in the middle of the sprawl of the University of Pittsburgh buildings in Oakland, Pennsylvania.

Alongside the Ohio River ran the Ohio River Boulevard and town after town until you came to the famous town of Sewickley, Pennsylvania where many Pittsburgh tycoons built their mansions. Next-door to Sewickley was a very small hamlet, Edgeworth, where I lived until I was nine years old. Our street ran perpendicular to the Ohio River Boulevard and shortly ended at a lovely little park in the shape of The Point, a triangle.

As a child this street was my world; bounded on either end, but seemingly endless. The trees, tall and shady in the summer seemed one hundred feet high, the houses were brick, or frame, and some were quite large from the Victorian era with long porches running around them. The yards were open in front, but most were fenced in back with gates on

13

Sandlot Stories

each side. Our neighbors typically had apple or peach trees and vegetable gardens.

It was a straight street with small side streets and alleys that ran behind our houses. Although we could ride our bicycles from one end to the other in five minutes and run it in ten to fifteen on our small feet; we often played a game of running the street by going in and out of each backyard through the gates and over the fences. This took much more time, but was a lot more exciting.

As a rule, children under six years old were kept inside or in the gated backyards under supervision. I was confined to our backyard with my sisters, which was completely fenced on one side and walled on the other three, so that my mother felt safe in allowing us to play there while she did her housework. My older sister and I soon learned to dig and tunnel our way out of the yard to freedom. We would go through the back alley and immerge on the street to our delight and my mother's dismay. Each time we did this my father would patiently fill in the hole and try to cover more of the wall with a bush, but we would eventually find another escape route. This routine was kept up for years. When my older sister was given the unattended freedom of the front yard, I determined to keep our tunneling and escape tradition going. I finally graduated to the austere privilege of the run of the street in 1964.

I was already a baseball fan before I even hit the front street. My father's father, my Papa, was quite old by then and would sit in a chair for hours listening to the Pirates' baseball games on the radio. We often went to see him and

Sandlot Stories

I would sit on the floor at his knee and listen to the games with him.

I learned many things from my grandfather. He was born in the 1880's and ran away from home at fifteen, lied about his age and went to The Spanish American War with Teddy Roosevelt. He then went out into the Western United States and became a marshal in a Western town. He showed me pictures of himself in cowboy dress with Indians wearing beads and full-feathered headdresses. He was wounded in the army in World War I and then settled back in Pittsburgh. At the beginning of the Great Depression, Papa had bought a farm so that he could be sure of feeding his family. When I was young, we went to Papa's farm to cut our Christmas trees. In my eyes he had led an exciting and heroic life, so when he also taught me that the greatest baseball team in the World was the Pittsburgh Pirates of the early 1960's—of course I listened!

At my Papa's knee, I learned about Roberto Clemente, Willy Stargell, Bill Mazeroski, Dick Groat, Vern Law, Don Williams, and others of the early '60's team. The best thing that ever happened in the whole world, according to Papa, was the 1960 World Series when Pittsburgh beat the New York Yankees. By the time I was allowed out onto the street, I was a little Pirate.

I was born pigeon-towed and had to wear corrective shoes until I was six years old. This may seem insignificant to you, but these were very clunky, very large, brown shoes. Although they did correct my feet and I was able to walk well in them, I could not run in them. When I was very young

Sandlot Stories

My Papa on His Farm with "Buddy"

Sandlot Stories

other kids would make fun of my sisters and me because all of us had this problem and these shoes. Magically though, the ugly, brown, orthopedic shoes came off at six years of age, and the back gate opened to let us into the front yard and the street. So, my graduation onto the street was more than just freedom from the backyard, it was freedom to run and run I did!

Most of the girls my age were playing "Barbies" or "dress up." Though I did participate in those games at times, I almost immediately fell in with the boys on our street. They were running and playing running games.

During the fall and winter months, we played games like "Combat" where the boys and a few of us girls, ran around diving into the street gutters, behind trees and bushes, and pretended to be at war with two teams. We also acted out books and stories that we knew into plays. These always involved running and "swash-buckling" as pirates or galloping on make-believe horses as "Cowboys and Indians." I was always an Indian complete with feathers and mud on my face.

During summer we played baseball. Across the street from my house and one door over was a vacant lot that was our baseball field. By the time I came to play, the children of the generations before me had run a dirt diamond permanently into the grass. We marked off first, second and third base with things like a rock, a large piece of cardboard box, or someone's shirt (much to the dismay of their mother). In the back of this field was a line of blackberry bushes that actually held fruit. These trees separated the lot from the

Sandlot Stories

backyard of the house on the next street behind it. On the sides were two houses, one with a fenced yard.

Home plate was a large tree that was on the side closest to the street in the corner next to the house without a fence. Our playing field faced out to the other house with the fence, so we often hit balls into this yard and someone had to jump the fence or run around to retrieve them. I don't remember anyone ever breaking a window, perhaps we were too little and not good enough at bat to break them.

Kids started showing up on the street in the late morning. Typically we would bike for a while in the morning or play other games. Our baseball game, or "The Game" would start in the afternoon sometime. We did not have organized teams, but picked them on the spur of the moment from the available line up of kids. The two oldest kids were the team leaders and they would take turns picking the rest of their team. Usually the youngest, or six year olds, were picked last and the odd man could stand in for any player on either team if that person was called by their mother to come inside.

After awhile I was not picked last because I could hit pretty well, although I was not a great catcher. I usually played at first base or right field. I liked right field best because I had more time to line up my eyesight on the ball. Also, if there was a dispute and the game stopped, I could sneak into the blackberry bushes and grab some berries to eat!

The kids on our street were all from immigrant families— the suburbs of Pittsburgh are known for their melting-pot populations; Irish, German, Italian, Polish, etc. The boys

Sandlot Stories

always settled disputes with a fight since we did not have an umpire. I was often the only girl playing ball, but was expected to fight like a boy. I think we made up a lot of our rules. We knew that each team got to hit until three people struck out and we should then change sides. We knew that the hitter stayed at bat until they were struck out and that someone was safe if they touched the base before the opposing player got them or the base with the ball. However, all the more subtle aspects of baseball were unknown to us and we fought a lot over rules according to the ideas of each player on any given day.

Being red-headed and of Irish and German descent, I was born with a bit of a temper. So, I can honestly say that if one of those boys said I was out, when I knew I was safe on a base, I had no problem raising my fists for a fight. However, my mother had a big problem with this as she wished I would spend my summers at the Edgeworth Country Club playing tennis and swimming and learning to be a "lady." Every time I came home from a fight I saw that look in her eye that silently said, "where have I failed with this one?" But it did not faze me, I was not going to be out when I was safe!

Everyone liked to slide into base in our games, just for the fun of getting dirty. We often slid when it was not neccessary and many of us worked at perfecting our "slide" technique. I loved to run around those bases and slide into them. It was such a feeling of freedom after my pigeon-towed walking as a young child.

When the Pirates played, we listened to the games on someone's radio. I remember sitting in a cool garage on

Sandlot Stories

a hot summer day and yelling at the radio as if we were at a game. My immediate family was not much interested in baseball so I did not go to the Pirates' games even though they were a half-hour drive away. Once my father took me to a Pirates' game when I was older at the new Three River's Stadium. That was the only major league game I saw until I was an adult and could go myself. The Pirates were playing St. Louis and it was a no-hitter for the Cardinals' pitcher. Although the Pirates lost, I got to see my heros and Roberto Clemente use his famous basket-catch in right field. I was thrilled!

On one of the side streets in our neighborhood was a house with very high shrubs completely surrounding it, so that the house could not even be seen from the street. I never saw any of my neighbors talking to the family in this house and did not know who lived there, but I did know that they were the only African-American family in the neighborhood. One day I was walking by their house and heard the Pirates' game on the radio. I wandered in through their driveway and met Bill. Bill was the grandfather and listening to the game seated in a lawn chair in their front yard. He had a big old dog sitting next to him and I asked if I could listen to the game with him. We became fast friends and I would come over often to hear the Pirates and talk over the game with him. I never asked anyone if I could go there—I just went. His daughter and son-in-law were very nice to me and I became a frequent visitor during summer, happy to have another grandfather just around the corner!

I moved from that street up into Sewickley proper and a

Sandlot Stories

Home Plate Tree On Our Sandlot

Sandlot Stories

prestigious home when I was nine. I never played sandlot ball after that but joined the youth tennis team at the Edgeworth club and learned to swim the length of their Olympic size pool in one breath. I went on to play on tennis teams for many years. In high school, when we lived in Cumberland, Maryland, our tennis team worked out with the baseball team. I secretly always wished I could run off to the baseball field after the workout, with that uniform on, rather than trot off to the tennis court to practice my serve.

I have raised my own kids on baseball. I will always remember those warm summer evenings when we wanted to get in one more inning before being called into dinner.

— Marcella

• • •

Roberto Clemente. #21 for the Pittsburgh Pirates, is my favorite baseball player of all time. In the 1960's, listening to the Pirates on the radio was so exciting because the announcers had so much emotion in their voices, particularly when Roberto Clemente would throw one of those bullet shots from the right field wall all the way into home base on one throw! Later, I admired him because he would say, "God wanted me to play baseball." I used to think about that. Then he died giving his life to be of service to others. He is a true hero.

Baseball Cards

In the summer of 1933, I was nine years old. My aunt invited me to my first big league baseball game. The Washington Senators were going to play our Chicago White Sox. From that day on I was hooked on baseball.

I began listening to baseball games on the radio and started collecting big league baseball cards. For a penny, you could get a two inch square piece of gum and a card depicting the players physical statistics and his career history. My collection grew to about three or four hundred cards.

The cards included such players as Babe Ruth, Lou Gehrig, Luke Appling (my favorite), and Carl Hubbell of the New York Giants. In 1934, Hubbell once struck out five consecutive power hitters in the second All-Star game played. I believe the five were none other than Babe Ruth, Lou Gehrig, Jimmie Foxx, Al Simmons, and Joe Cronin.

There were other cards of not so famous players, nonetheless, interesting. Such players as Chick Hafey, the first professional to wear glasses, and Moe Berg who spoke several languages and was considered the smartest man ever to play the game. Who could forget those relatively unknowns with names like Eppa Rixey and "Ki Ki" Kieler.

One card that I always wanted but was never able to get was Johnny Vander Meer who pitched for the Cincinnati Reds. Vander Meer was the only pitcher to throw two consecutive no hitters, he did it in 1939 in the first night

Sandlot Stories

game ever played at Ebbets Field against the Brooklyn Dodgers, beating them 6-0.

In 1983, the fiftieth anniversary of the cards, I sold them and with them went a chapter in my life that I have always cherished.

— Harry Cavey

Baseball Heaven

My biggest thrill in baseball came in the summer of 1940. The Chicago Cubs announced they were going to conduct a one day baseball clinic. Space was limited, and hundreds wanted to attend, so the organization had the kids fill out applications and told us we would be notified if selected. With great anticipation I awaited an answer. Within a few days I received a letter requesting me to report to Wrigley Field.

Upon arriving at the park, along with a few dozen other kids, we were told to go to the locker room and select an old Cub's uniform. The uniform that I chose had once belonged to Augie Galan, an outfielder. We then went out to the field and began a workout drill, the coaches had us going through the fundamentals of hitting, fielding, throwing, and running the bases.

When I took my position at second base, I thought how thrilling it was to be where many great players had performed. I looked at the smooth and beautiful field with grass instead of cinders and no stones to deflect a ground ball. There were real bases instead of the crushed cans or pieces of cardboard we had used on the lots. Truly for one brief day, all of us kids were in baseball heaven.

— Harry Cavey

Sandlot Stories

Playing For Our Own Pride

Growing up in Austin, Minnesota, baseball was always a major part of our community. George A. Hormel, the meatpacking company, was headquartered there and in the 1940's and 1950's sponsored a semi-pro baseball team which in the summers was the main form of entertainment for the town of 22,000 people. There was no television in the '40's so my earliest memories were going to the baseball park to watch my father play on the Hormel team. My Dad grew up on a farm in Iowa and played baseball in high school. He came to Austin to stay with relatives and look for a job. After being encouraged to try out for the Hormel team, he was selected as an outfielder/first baseman but still with no job. In his first game, he got two doubles and a single and the next day he was working at Hormel's where he worked for thirty-nine years as a steamfitter.

I share this background to help you understand that my baseball roots go deep. I grew up in a neighborhood of twelve boys, all within about two to four years of each other, so we had all the ingredients for a summer of baseball at the park down the street.

It was not an ideal baseball field but it was ours and we made the best of it. The park was shaped like an irregular trapezoid. The left field line was bordered by a street so that we had to be careful of cars when fielding any foul popup. Foul territory down the right field line also contained some

Sandlot Stories

fielding challenges since it was defined by the high bank of Turtle Creek. The "Creek" in its rambling actually came fairly close to the road thereby defining the point of the trapezoid which was where we established home plate. Left field had the only fence which ran the length of the neighbor's yard, all the way to dead center field. Behind the fence was a tall row of cottonwood trees which formed our own version of the "green monster." Right field was open all the way to the driveway of the one house that sat on the bank of the creek.

While being somewhat irregular, our field was not unlike many others except for the playground equipment in left field. Left field was the shortest part of the park and it was where the city fathers decided to install playground equipment in the form of a swing set, teeter totter, slide, sand box and a garbage can. As a result, deployment of our outfielders went from being routine to a major strategic decision. Speed and quickness became important in being able to navigate the obstacles in left field.

However, none of that mattered much back then since we played baseball every day—rain or shine. The two oldest boys in the neighborhood were always captains since at ten years old, they were physically bigger and stronger then the rest of us. I was six years old in 1948 when I began playing with these guys. I was tall for my age and skinny as a rail but having started early playing catch with my Dad, I could hold my own catching, throwing and hitting. Once the teams were picked, one of the captains would throw a bat in the air to the other captain who would catch it in one hand. The

Sandlot Stories

two captains would then go hand over hand until one of them would grip the knob of the bat. This would determine who was up to bat first. It was a ritual repeated daily for the six years I played in that park.

Occasionally, we would not have all of the boys available to play so we would play a game called two batter work up. Basically, two boys would start out as batters and the rest would be in the field. The objective was to continue to bat without making an out. If lucky, the batter could bat for a long time but whoever made the out would go to the field and the person pitching would become the batter. The person who made the out would go to the outfield and the rotation would continue from outfield to third base to shortstop to first base to pitcher until becoming the batter. The great part of this game was that we could play it with only five kids if we used the bicycles as a back stop instead of a catcher.

Due to the physical layout of the field, first base became the most critical position on the field because it was the only opportunity we had to stop the ball, usually our only ball, from going down the bank into the creek. While we rarely lost a ball to the creek, there were days when the ball became very heavy by the end of the day as a result of numerous errant throws to first. The one advantage of playing first during the heat of the day was that we could quickly jump down the bank of the creek to take a deep drink from the little spring that trickled into the creek. The water was always cool and sweet and as I remember it, the best drink of water I ever had.

The games were always spirited as we played without hats

Sandlot Stories

or shirts and became a deep bronze early in the season. The only issues I can remember were when the Burton brothers were on different teams. It seems that on occasion they would end up in a wrestling match when one or the other would slide into a base too hard colliding with his brother. After the brief skirmish, the game would pick up again and continue until we were all called to dinner.

It was a time of the purist form of competition with boys playing for their own pride with no parents intervening, no umpires and rules made up on the fly by boys who knew the game. Everyone played because they wanted to and not because they were forced to by a parent trying to relive their own childhood. It was a time of innocence in the sense that nothing else mattered beyond playing baseball and developing our skills. There were no car pools, no uniforms, no fans just baseball played for the love of the game. I know we were all the better as a result.

Baseball served as a catalyst to play other sports which in my case were basketball and football. I was fortunate to grow up at a time of many good athletes and our teams enjoyed great success in high school. I graduated in 1960 and was all-state in football, basketball and baseball. Getting the early start in baseball no doubt helped me to develop in the other sports. In July of 1960 I signed a professional baseball contract with the Philadelphia Phillies. While my baseball career was cut short by an injury, I never lost my love of the game or forgot the lessons of hard work, team play, and camaraderie that baseball afforded me growing up.

— *By Clayton Reed*

Sandlot Stories

• • •

I grew up being a Milwaukee Braves fan since it was the closest team to Minnesota. My favorite player was Henry Aaron, number 44. I loved him because he was a complete player. While known for his home runs later in his career, I admired the fact that he could run, throw and play an outstanding right field with little or no fan fare. He was the consummate professional in his demeanor and work ethic. It was a great time to grow up with baseball in the 1950's because the game was still relatively untainted and the talent was exceptional.

— Clayton Reed

Sandlot Stories

My Tractor Field

I grew up on a farm in central California. We had many fruit trees and the peaches were good practice for throwing the ball. I would take a peach and try to aim it at a tree trunk, a branch, or the wheel of a tractor. When I would get a "strike" I was rewarded with the fruit exploding into many pieces.

Ours was a modern farm where I got to drive the tractors, forklifts, and hauled the fruit and vegetables on a truck to the packing sheds or the shippers. We did do things later at night to irrigate or to haul in the fruit that was picked during the day. It took time to make multiple trips to the place were we delivered the fruit. I would unload it and return to get the boxes that were left at the farm. Although I did not have to get up at the crack of dawn, this work did consume a lot of the day.

My brother and I would play when the work was over. The times in-between work at the farm gave me opportunity to throw peaches at things to see if I could hit my target. But usually we would play near sunset. This was at the end of the day when things were done. It was hot in the afternoons, ninety degrees or in the low one-hundred's, and there was the afternoon work to do, so the cool evening before sunset was our time.

Our place to play was in front of our house. The house was situated away from the main country road and was at a ninety-

Sandlot Stories

degree angle from the road. There was a long driveway where the house was at the left, the various equipment on the right, and continuing on down the driveway was a shed for farm equipment and working on things, another small house (an old house my folks first lived in and later my grandmother) and eventually, the orchards. The orchards surrounded the back of the house and the other side of the equipment area. So we played in the driveway.

The dirt in the driveway was hard since oil was put on it to make it less dusty. But the area where the equipment was kept had soft dirt, especially during the summer. Here, a fly ball would bounce if it hit the oiled part of the driveway but would die in the soft, dusty dirt in the other area. A baseball mitt could easily get this dirt in the finger slots and you would have to shake the dust and dirt off. There were a few big trees along the driveway so they too could be hit by the ball. This was our playing field.

I would often play "three-flys-up" in the yard with my brother and neighborhood friends. Our playing field, with all its many different pieces of farm equipment sprinkled around and other obstacles was a challenge. There were times when we had to catch the ball balancing on a tractor-trailer or run after a ground ball that had ricocheted off equipment in the yard. This had the added advantage of honing our skills for anticipating the direction of the ball and improving our coordination. It is a good practice technique—highly recommended!

We did do other things around our farm for fun. We were creative since we didn't go anywhere else. There was an

34

irrigation ditch where we would swim and in one area went water skiing. Our water skiing consisted of a Volkswagen driving on the ditchbank with a rope tied to the back and then a flat wooden board as the ski that you stood on at an angle. The tricky part was getting around the bend in the ditch and avoiding the ditchbank.

But I loved to practice baseball even when by myself. I used a large plywood board that I leaned up between two garage doors and threw a tennis ball against it. The corners of the plywood, the imperfections in the wood, or areas outside the plywood would cause the ball to bounce in unpredictable ways. So the fun of playing this way was in fielding the ball, throwing it back against the plywood and getting the out.

When I was in third grade, both of my front teeth were accidentally broken from a baseball bat. This really affected me so that afterwards I was always afraid of the ball, particularly in fast pitch baseball. I was afraid that it would hit my teeth and break them again.

When some friends challenged older kids to a game they all wanted to play fast pitch with a hard ball. When I got up to bat the pitcher said he was going to throw his "coffin" ball. When the ball left his hand it came right at me. I was able to turn away from it in time for it to nail me in the back. I knew for sure then that I would never be able to play fast pitch ball.

I enjoyed playing slow pitch softball. When I was growing up playing and watching others, I decided that the important thing about batting was to get on base so that I could score

Sandlot Stories

more runs. Most kids wanted to hit the home run but would fly out. I concentrated on the basics of getting solid hits.

With this practice I was able in later years to place the ball in just about any area of the field. I ended up getting a number of home runs since I could place the ball in the hole between center and right field. In the games I played, the worst player would usually be in right field since most players hit right handed. That's where I would hit the ball. Many times, with even the worst player, the ball would go directly to them and they would get the lucky catch. But when I aimed to the hole between center and right field I could usually get it past the fielders and get a home run.

The only way I could play fast pitch ball was when a tennis ball or ping-pong ball was used. The ping-pong ball was fun since you could get nice curve balls with it.

When I was about five years old, I remember I was in town one day and some older bullies came up to me. One kid looked at me, grabbed my shirt, and asked me if I was a Giants' or Dodgers' fan. Being from central California there was a mix of San Francisco Giants' and Los Angeles Dodgers' fans. When the bully asked me whose side I was on I didn't understand what a "giant" or a "dodger" was. He told me from now on I was a Giants' fan or he would beat me up.

To this day I have always been a Giants' fan and fortunately I moved to the bay area for my job instead of Los Angeles.

— Dean
Kingsburg, California

Sandlot Stories

. . .

I didn't have a favorite player that I followed. I just enjoyed playing. Although, I remember an advertisement with Willie Mays that I had seen as a kid that sticks in my mind. He was warning kids not to touch blasting caps that must have been around construction sites in San Francisco. I never understood the commercial as a kid but just remember the phrase he kept saying, "Don't tuuuuj dem" (or don't touch them) while in the background it showed his famous over the head catch and in another version of the commercial it showed when he threw out someone tagging up from third on a fly ball and Mays' throw got him out at home.

— *Dean*

Sandlot Stories

Cricket Or Softball?

When I grew up in India, which was many years back in the 1960's, neither baseball nor softball was a game that kids played. I lived in the city of Madras, located in the southern part of India, and there were two schools in Madras that offered softball as one of the games played during the Physical Education (PE) period. I was attending one of these schools and thus introduced to softball.

We played softball on a soccer field using bases. No one used gloves of any kind to catch the ball. Since we were used to catching a cricket ball (a cricket ball is as hard as a baseball and very similar in size and design) using bare hands, catching the softball was not an issue.

We did not have coaches. Our PE teacher told us the general way to play the game. By the time we picked up the equipment and walked over to the field, we usually had only thirty-five minutes left. We used the same "four balls with three strikes" rule. We formed two teams and created our own rules to fit into a forty-five minute PE period. These made-up rules varied from grade to grade. Some other students followed the rules of the game more closely and usually completed three full innings. But, in our class, each team batted until all the players had a chance to bat, barely finished one inning. Therefore, the games our class played were always one inning long.

Sandlot Stories

Cricket, soccer and field hockey were the popular games that were played between schools. Softball was a game for the PE period. Since softball was not a college sport, we never looked at it as anything other than a fun PE sport. In team sports, kids were serious about cricket, soccer and field hockey

Later, in my senior year in high school, softball was introduced as an inter-school competitive sport for the first time. A few of the people from the cricket team were automatically placed on the softball team. That was an interesting experience playing the game again with the cricket players.

After coming to the United States, watching baseball brought me back to my old memories of softball in my middle/high school. However, the strategies stomped me at first, because we never played it the way it is played here. Now, with my kids playing baseball, it has drawn me into it. I enjoy watching my kids play the game with other kids and going to the major league ball games with them.

— *Ravi*

Big League Stars

When I was a boy in the mid 1960's growing up in Los Angeles County, we rode our bikes down to Citrus College with our mitts hanging on our handlebars. We would pick teams by one captain throwing the bat in the air and the other captain catching it and then they would each proceed with alternating hands—one on top of the other moving towards the nob of the bat. When the last person had covered the nob of the bat, that team had won the right to be up first to bat. We would play until our chest hurt from the L.A. smog, take a break, go for a swim, and meet back after dinner to resume the game.

In the 1970's when we moved up from Southern California to Northern California, our game resumed once again without missing a beat. This time we had a baseball field in the front yard of our house. We lived across the street from a court that ended in a churchyard at the back of the court. The churchyard had a tall fence, which we used as our "home run fence." At the front of the court, home plate was spray painted onto the street as well as second base. The street light pole was the foul line down the right field line; the neighbor's chimney was the foul pole for the left field line. The light pole also gave us the added benefit of being able to have night games as well. We used wooden bats and tennis balls so we wouldn't break any windows.

Everyone would always try to "go yard", which meant

Sandlot Stories

trying to hit a home run (into the church yard). We got three swinging strikes and no walks were allowed. At other times we just had "home run" derbys into the church yard. Once in awhile one of us would get off a real good shot straight into center that would hit the church. This was no easy task getting it between the trees and the houses.

Some of my fondest childhood memories were playing baseball with my friends. I think some of the best games played were when there weren't any adults around to enforce our rules or behavior. Then we played with all our heart and were all big league stars!

My love of baseball was always deep in my roots. From a very young age I had heard about my Grandpa. He had played semi-pro ball in the Ohio League as a catcher. He had the highest batting average on the Ashland Ohio City Team. His cousin was also a catcher in the 1930's for the Yankees with Babe Ruth! Imagine having these legends right in your own family! Of course I loved baseball and of course when I played sandlot ball—I was my Grandpa all over again!

— *Donny*

Donny's Grandpa On The Garber Team
Sponsored by Great-Grandpa and
Garber Printing

Sandlot Stories

Grandmothers Can Play Baseball Too!

One day while I was visiting my grandchildren, who eat, sleep, and live to play baseball, I was asked if I had ever played baseball when I was their age. Silence. All three pairs of little eyes gazed at me, anxiously awaiting my answer. I'm sure it was hard for them to visualize Grandma playing baseball.

I told them a little bit about my childhood days growing up in the little coastal town of Santa Barbara, California. It was the period after the big stock market crash and before World War II. Many people I knew were out of work. Those who had jobs worked long hours, seven days a week, at menial jobs. Many of us were from single-parent families and were expected to fend for ourselves at an early age. Besides the routine things like getting ourselves ready for school, eating and doing our homework, we learned to do chores and entertain ourselves. We made up games and improvised for our fun. Santa Barbara was a beautiful city with beautiful parks and beaches, but we could go only as far as our legs would take us.

Our neighborhood was comprised of Chinese, Japanese, Italian and Mexican families. It was an opportunity to learn about the cultures and customs of families from other countries.

My family rented a two-bedroom unit in "Chinatown." Santa Barbara Chinatown was only a block long. There

Sandlot Stories

weren't that many Chinese families…mostly old, single men who had come over to work helping to build the railroad. These men were not allowed to bring their wives and children to join them in the "Land of the Golden Mountain."

We had a community backyard for all the apartment units. It consisted of a large, hard dirt area for parking. Because most of the people could not afford a car, some of the renters used the space to grow their own vegetables. Others raised pigeons and rabbits. We raised chickens. I helped feed them. It was fascinating watching the chickens lay eggs. There weren't enough eggs to go around, so it was a special treat when it was my turn to fetch the nice, warm, fresh eggs and choose one for myself. I enjoyed watching my egg cook, knowing that it will end up in my tummy…fresh and yummy!

The children needed a place to play, so what was left of the remaining dirt area, we claimed as our playground. We wanted our playing field to be safe. There was much work to be done. The potholes needed to be filled with small rocks to avoid getting sprained ankles. Rusted nails had to be picked up. We needed to do something about the dust. We did not have a hose with a sprayer. That would have been fast, easy, and fun. We used whatever we could find…empty jars, small cans, or paper cups... to carry the water to sprinkle on the dust. The older boys used buckets. Sometimes I pulled and pushed the heavy buckets of water, but more water splashed on me than on the ground! I discovered that the puddle of water I spilled made that spot soft and muddy. I found a stick to stir the squishy mud puddle. It was fun! I

Sandlot Stories

could make all sorts of things …like mud pies for everyone! I was about five-years old at the time.

Our equipment consisted of one big bat. It was too heavy for me to use, so my brother made a small bat out of an old broomstick for me. I soon learned that sprained fingers, sprained ankles, and skinned knees were part of the perils of playing baseball with the older kids. Our ages ranged from five to thirteen years…mostly boys played. There was no special time that we played. Whenever any of us finished our chores and homework, we would go to our playground. Weekends were the best time. We took turns being pitcher and batter if there were only two of us. We never kept score. Because I was a girl and only five years old, a few of the boys said a strike was only when my bat made contact with the ball. The rules changed depending on who showed up to play. Often times I was "asked" not to play. One time a boy brought some oranges "just for the fun of it" because there were no balls. What a squishy mess! Yuk!

Our bases were parts of cardboard boxes or pieces of paper with rocks piled on top. We mostly just needed one base. A long driveway came into our "baseball field." We tried to set up a roadblock with boxes because the delivery trucks used the driveway as a shortcut. The drivers would run over the boxes and yell at us, but I didn't understand a word they were saying. One day I happened to repeat some of those English words to my family that I had been hearing. Boy, did I get a scolding! It was like a thunderstorm coming down! Even though my father spoke very little English, he evidently knew what those words meant. Those were *Very*

Sandlot Stories

Bad Words and I was *Never To Repeat Them Again!*

Older boys (junior high and high school age) often times came and "borrowed" our bat. It didn't take them long to break mine. Their balls would hit the sides of the apartment houses so close to the windows that the people would come out and scold us. A few threatened to call the police. Those hits were considered an "out." Sometimes the ball was hit so hard, it went over the wall to the back of the post office and hit someone or something. We could hear people's angry voices. Balls going over the wall were considered "homeruns." I didn't understand why, after making a homerun, the older boys would run away and give me the bat.

Those boys would play until they lost our ball. We little kids spent most of our time looking for the balls. Sometimes the balls went into the "jungle"…an area with old dying trees and overgrown, prickly bushes. Inside the jungle lived a mean old man with a long beard like Rip Van Winkle. He had mean looking eyes, brown stained teeth, and growled at us. He would hold a big stick up and dare us to come get our balls. I was sent in to get the ball while the others distracted him. It didn't work! I ran as fast as my little legs would go as the old man lowered the stick. I wasn't badly hurt, but I was badly scared! I had nightmares for a long time after that.

My love of playing baseball continued into junior high and high school. The best girl players in our high school were chosen to play softball against the faculty at the end of the school year. That was our school's tradition. What an honor

Sandlot Stories

it was to be captain of the all girls' team. My teachers were surprised to see me out in the field pitching to them. I was equally surprised to see some of my more reserved women teachers playing. The male teachers kept teasing me during the game, as I was only ninety-eight pounds at the time, and the faculty members didn't think I could throw hard enough to get the ball across home plate.

Thank goodness my guardian angel was there for me. I was pitching one of my best games. I swung the bat with every ounce of energy in my body and managed to hit a few homeruns for our team. In class the next morning, one of the teachers laughingly called me by the name "Slugger." My teammates were the real Sluggers who won the game! We had great fun playing against our own teachers with the student body watching and cheering us on. I had the opportunity to see another side of my teachers and they saw another side of me. We bonded that day. Our friendship continued long after I graduated.

Eddie Matthews, who was one of my classmates, was there along with most of the school watching us play. He hadn't spoken to me up until that day when the ball I hit sailed high over his head for my first homerun. He looked shocked! Then he grinned and clapped and cheered us on. I used to watch Eddie play after school. One time, one of his homerun hits came straight at me. Luckily it was my thumb that broke and not my head. I couldn't get out of the way of his "lightning fast" ball.

Our high school graduation dance was a memorable experience filled with excitement. As my date and I

Sandlot Stories

entered, we found the place swarming with photographers and baseball agents. My date, a city boy from out-of-town, didn't know what was going on! After all, it was just a high school graduation dance. Is this what happens when people from a small town graduate, he wondered? But the rest of us knew why the agents and photographers were there. The agents had been following Eddie Matthews for days. Some even pushed their way onto the dance floor. Eddie wanted to stay to enjoy his graduation night with his date and with his classmates. Under the circumstances, it was impossible to do so. How could we "save" Eddie and be rid of these intruders who were disrupting our special night? Brainstorm: Hide Eddie in a safe place...the girls' bathroom! Have a group of girls block the entrance to the bathroom and scream, if necessary. Eddie can escape by crawling through the bathroom window to a car that was waiting for him outside. Mission successful!

From watching Eddie play, seeing the scouts in the stands, we all knew Eddie would realize his dream of becoming a professional baseball player. The last time most of us saw Eddie Matthews was at our 50th Class Reunion.

I am so happy my grandchildren are having fun playing baseball, making lots of new friends, and collecting baseball cards. Yes, my little ones, Grandmas can play baseball too!

— Grandma

Baseball Was Baseball

I must have been in third or fourth grade, somewhere around nine or ten years old when my older brother and I would spend our Saturday morning's playing a pick-up game with our neighborhood buddies. That was all there was to do during those days, besides watching Saturday morning cartoons. We would walk down to our local Catholic school with our friends. Our field was the grass lot in the back of our Catholic grade school in Houston, Texas. It was nothing special and was probably covered in mud most of the time, since it rained so much in Houston. We didn't care, baseball was baseball.

We played a version of work up, where we took turns batting and running, while people rotated up from different positions on the field. I wasn't very good at baseball, but nobody cared. It was memorable because we just played for fun, and everyone got to play and get dirty.

Afterwards, grime and all, we would walk down to the nearest corner drug store, and plop down our nickel (or dime?) and get a cherry phosphate drink. We were like bulls in a china closet, with all our dirty clothes and milling around all the finery in a drug store sipping our drinks. It's a wonder they even let us in the place.

My favorite team in Houston was the old Colt 45's, soon to be the Houston Astros. I can remember my older cousin, who drove, taking us to the new Astrodome stadium at the

Sandlot Stories

time it was being built. That was exciting. You can imagine the excitement because it was the first dome stadium ever built for baseball or any sport. It cost something like thirteen million dollars to build, which sounds like peanuts now!

I still remember the first time I went to a game when it opened, how impressed I was. You can't describe the grandiosity of seeing a baseball field under a dome. It was the largest enclosed space I had ever seen and it just awed everyone when they arrived inside.

— Rene W.
Houston, Texas

Big Brothers

When it came to playing pickup games in Escalon, California it was a first come, first served basis for the field. Even when adults came to play softball on the diamond we would tell them to get lost if we had gotten there first. Of course they were older and bigger and we really only had problems once or twice where we were outmatched and had to give up the field. The good thing about Escalon back then, was that it was such a small town that we pretty much knew everyone. No one pays attention to kids so retaliation for getting kicked off the field meant we knew who's car was going to get egged the next week.

All of the fields were at the schools and were well taken care of by the school custodians, though the backstops were often in bad shape. There were no bases around the diamond but a square drawn in the dirt was good enough. We had most of the normal rules except for pitching, which was supplied by our own team. This made it easy to hit and made it more exciting for the outfielders.

We played baseball all day long and our only time limit was the sun going down. Then it was time to play ditch or go home. Otherwise, when one game ended we would just mix up players and play another game. The teams were divided evenly or I wouldn't have gotten to play at all. My brother and his friends are four years older than my friends and me, so balanced teams were necessary.

Sandlot Stories

I can only remember my Dad playing catch with me once or twice. I don't remember him ever coming to any of my games but he didn't go to the games my brothers played either. He was very supportive of us but just never made it to the baseball games. This was weird because he never missed any of my archery tournaments that were held during those same years that I was playing baseball, just at different times of the year.

Besides our regular baseball games, we used to have wiffle ball games in our front yard on a regular basis. Originally, our road was a dead end and then it was widened to a through street. Even for the few years that it was a dead end, we were still forbidden to play in the road. So, the wiffle ball game was always in the yard.

Home plate was a dip in the front yard, first base was the plum tree, second was a rose bush, third was the corner post of the front porch. If we could hit it past the mailboxes it was a home run. If it went in the street or over the neighbor's fence it was an out.

The wiffle ball games were made up of almost every kid in the neighborhood, except there were no girls in this neighborhood that had any interest in wiffle ball or our baseball games.

Whenever we didn't have enough people to play a regular baseball game we always had enough for work-ups. In our work up games we had to pick which two outfields we were going to hit to. If the ball didn't make it out of the infield or if we hit it to the opposite field it was an out. First base became the pitchers mound and a throw to the mound before

Sandlot Stories

the runner made it to first base was declared an out. Only three people could be up at a time. If all three loaded the bases, the guy on third would call for a ghost runner and then take his next at bat. The catch was that the guy on second had to make it to third before the ball made it back to the pitcher's mound or the ghost runner would be called out at home.

Although I played on farms and worked on my grandparents' farm growing up, I never played baseball or wiffle ball on a farm. And, even though my Dad never made it to my games, all of my grandparents and my mom made it to most of the games.

None of us were exceptional players, we only played for the fun of the game. Some of us had better throwing arms, some were better pitchers, some were good hitters and some were good at hitting homeruns if they ever hit the ball.

Growing up in this area allowed us to play many sports like football, golf, bike riding, and I can even remember swimming across the Stanislaus River with my fishing pole and tackle box tied around me. I should have sunk like an anchor but I made it there and back on more than one occasion with my friends. After all, the best fishing was always in the places that were inaccessible or private property.

But the one memory that sticks out more than my blue baseball glove is that it was so terribly hot. We played here in the valley in the middle of the summer and anyone who has spent a summer here knows what I am talking about. Sometimes I think the only reason I went to the games was for the cold sodas afterwards.

Sandlot Stories

I did play little league for a few years here in Escalon and there was a team in Collegeville that we played. Three of the schools were in walking distance from our house. There were at least two baseball fields at every school in the Escalon Unified School District but because of the expansion of this area only a few are left.

For most of my little league playing days I was the catcher for the team. I don't know if the manager chose me because I was the fattest and he wanted a backstop or if I had a good enough arm to throw to second. Whatever the reason, I don't care. All I know is that I hated being catcher and getting a baseball in the groin from time to time and getting run over at home plate.

I never made it to the playoffs on any of the teams I was on but we did finish second in our division once. It was tough because my older brother was always on a winning team that walked away with huge trophies after winning every game they played.

When I got into the seventh or eighth grade I found it much more fun playing baseball with friends and relatives from the neighborhood on a weekly and sometimes daily basis. I never tried out for the teams in high school because again, I had more fun with a loose schedule of playing when friends wanted to and I didn't have to be the catcher.

My older brother is the one that got me started in collecting baseball cards. He is four years older than me and I was just his kid brother that had to stay out of his way. When I was lucky, I use to get to watch him trade baseball cards with his friend on the bedroom floor. The rules were simple, I must

Sandlot Stories

stay motionless and not make a peep and I could stay. It was so interesting for me since I was only five or six years old and anything my big brother was interested in, I was interested in. When I was seven my Mom and Grandma took me to the toy store and bought me some baseball cards and I took them home, opened them, put them away and forgot about them. That was in 1977 and by 1982 I started my Reggie Jackson collection.

— Dave Sutton or "Dead"

• • •

My nickname growing up was "Dead". All my friends called me this because I was shy and kept to myself most of the time. They thought that I resembled the walking dead and the nickname stayed with me from grammer school through most of high school.

• • •

As for my favorite player—it would have to be Reggie Jackson who wore #9 for the Oakland A's. I didn't start collecting items with Reggie on them until 1977 or '78. Even then I didn't go out of my way to collect, until 1982—'83,

Sandlot Stories

when he was approaching his 500th home run. Although I should have stopped collecting years ago I find it is one of my favorite hobbies today.

I enjoyed watching Reggie at bat, waiting for that big swing not knowing if it would be a strike out or homer. When we played work ups I would try to do everything he did. We would even play on the girls' softball field so we could hit home runs a lot easier. It was all about the home run for me and Reggie was one of the best at it.

Dave on the Sutton Team
Sponsored by his Dad and Grandfather

Sandlot Stories

A Prize Just For Playing

In June, 1945 my father was an officer with General McArthur on his way to Japan. He and others of the Military Government Team boarded troop transport ships and sailed for the invasion of the Japanese homeland. On the way over Japan surrendered.

My mother, my brother and I were still living near the Japanese language school in Monterey when he left, at a place called Asilomar. The whole resort was filled with women and children whose fathers were spared an invasion of Japan. Dad was assigned to the 5th Amphibious Marine Corps as a member of their planned assault at Kagoshima, near Nagasaki. Instead they just walked ashore without a shot. This was possible because the Emperor of Japan, after the two bombs, asked the people to accept the end of the war and to cooperate with the United States Forces as they occupied the country.

Back in California we were jumping up and down, happy and Mom was crying. We had no mail from Dad for months so that no hint of the plans for the final invasion could be accidentally revealed. In a few weeks letters began to arrive from Dad and he told us of his adventures in that very foreign place.

One day a wooden box arrived, stuffed with wood shavings and a lacquer bowl and a teapot with six cups. I wasn't interested in the contents—the box and the wood

Sandlot Stories

shavings smelled so good. A smell I had never known. My imagination went full speed trying to see the place that could make a packing box smell so intriguing.

In a few months Dad said his work would take a few years and he didn't want to be there without us and would we like to live in Japan. We were eager to go right then but had to wait until the next summer to board the ship with American families. Our's was one of the "first ships" in 1946 to bring the wives and children from the United States to be reunited with their fathers in Japan who were staying on for the reconstruction. The ship was the Matson liner "Monterey."

Just before dawn August 11, 1945 a strangely familiar beautiful smell came in through the open porthole. It was that wood smell, sandalwood, that I had first smelled many months ago. We were at anchor in Yokohama harbor waiting for daylight and to dock.

As a young boy I can't remember playing baseball until I arrived in Japan in 1946. In a few weeks upon our arrival someone in charge of publicity thought it would be a good idea for the army to get up a baseball game between the American kids and the Japanese kids. For the Americans it was a bad idea because the teams were not well matched. I think few of us Americans had played much before that time and we were beaten.

I was ten years old, almost eleven. Every player was given a small prize which I learned was the custom in other sporting events in Japan. I think the prize was a new white rubber baseball. Winning wasn't the object of the game. I don't think the winner or the winning team was given special recognition. The object of the game was playing and being a member. This was my introduction into baseball.

We soon moved to Fukuoka where my younger brother and I were the only American children in town. My Dad bought a bicycle for me and I was encouraged to ride anywhere I wanted and learn my way around the city. My brother and I were viewed with great curiosity and kindness by the local citizens. How many times did we hear "*kawaii so ne!*" which means "poor guy" or sympathy for us. My best friend was the son of our landlord, Mr. Ito, a Shinto priest, who owned several homes.

We moved into his house and he and his family moved into another house. I was eleven years old and did not know the details of the appropriation of the Ito house but the son, my age, and I played together well. He had a pet cricket in a small cage and a nightingale.

Five or six years later while we were living in Okinawa I attended a baseball game. The champion New York Giants from the U.S. had come to Okinawa to play a local U.S. army team. It was one of those exhibition games for the benefit of the troops. Dad, Mom and my two younger brothers and I went to see them play.

I'm not even sure if they played nine innings, not that it mattered one way or another. The game took place at one of the army baseball fields. At least it had all the markings of a baseball field.

Our seats were along the first base line right across from the first baseman. During the game a ball hit down the first base line foul; I got up and grabbed the ball. While I was

Sandlot Stories

enjoying and relishing my accomplishment, Mom dampened the moment by suggesting I go over to the Giants' players to have them autograph the ball.

I was reluctant, bashful, a little shy or maybe all of the above and did not see this as something that I particularly cared to do. But, as the obedient oldest sibling I listened to Mom's orders and reluctantly headed over to the Giants' players with my ball. I remember Leo Durocher signing the middle spot on the ball. Than the ball was passed around to all the other Giants' players to sign. That ball was to remain in my possession for the next forty years.

When I found out my new son-in-law was a baseball fan, I dug out that old baseball from one of my drawers. It probably has not been looked at or touched since that day. He carefully examined the signatures against a book he had showing what their signatures looked like. That's how we realized the ball was from around the early 1950's.

We were trying to figure out who was on the Giants' team at that time, even though I don't think all the players participated in the trip to Japan. I think we concluded it was 1951. He came across one signature in particular; the player was George Spencer that did not look right. He looked at other sample signatures of George's and it still didn't look like it could have been his signature. Yet, all the other signatures matched perfectly.

I took one look at the signature and realized what had happened. I must have missed a signature and Mom had taken the program and added George's signature onto the ball!   — *Jim W.*

Was Just Fun

I remember as a little boy playing *kusa-yakyu*. My mother was very strict and wanted me to think only of going to school and of studying after school. My father liked to watch the professional baseball game of the Dragons on TV, but I was not interested because it was boring. To be able to play *kusa-yakyu* was just fun!

I was nine or ten years old when I played, mostly after that you join an organized team in Japan. My *kusa-yakyu* field was in a park by our house in Nagoya, Japan. I was lucky because I could walk to the park and still see my house from it.

After school everyday my neighborhood friends would gather at the field. We would usually have six people show up to play *kusa-yakyu*. One friend always brought the bat, but if we had no bat we used a stick from a tree root. I would bring a ball, sometimes we used a softball because it is much easier to hit. Everyone brought their own glove.

We didn't often have four bases. Most of the time we had three bases: home, first, and third. We drew bases either in the sand, used a corrugated board, or even used an old tire.

Our field now looks small, but as a child it seemed very big. There was grass in the middle, big trees on the 1st base side, sand on the 3rd base side and more big trees along the fence in the outfield. If you hit the ball over the fence into the road (which was a little road for one car only) it was a

Sandlot Stories

home run.

Each team had three players. Offense had to supply their own catcher. Defense had a pitcher, first base, and outfield. Before the start of each game we picked teams by doing "*Jyan-Ken*" (rock—*Goo*, Scissors—*Choky*, Paper—*Pa*) using only Goo and Choky. It didn't matter who won or lost the game. I only remember one time when we kept a scoreboard in the sand and made innings. We just played as long as we could, maybe four, five, or six innings.

It mattered more who hit a home run. I never hit a home run, but my friend who was one year older was the best player and often hit home runs. In Japan, in elementary school, we were all the same size so there was not much physical difference. The best player was not the biggest or the one who had the most physical strength, but the one that had more technique and good "timing."

In *kusa-yaku* there was no one there to make sure we had good manners, like in the organized baseball at school. Also in my *kusa-yaku* we had no *Gaki-Daisyo* (Gaki-Die-Show) or bully player like I see sometimes in other games—we just had fun!

When I played organized ball the only position the team let me play was catcher. This could have been because I was the fattest and didn't run fast. Also, there were other, better players in those other positions. It didn't matter to me the position I played because it was more important that I got to play! I didn't mind being the catcher because I had made up my mind to thinking that my position was very important—the most important, in fact! So I felt very good about it. I would be the best catcher that I could be. It was more important just to play.

— Taka or "Taka-Chan"

• • •

My close friends called me Taka-Chan—that was my nickname at the time and I liked being called that.

• • •

My favorite team is the Chunich Dragons—home team of Nagoya, Japan. This team has won a championship about once in ten years, but I was happy because they won the year I was born!

Sandlot Stories

Southwood 500

When we were kids and did not have enough kids for two full teams or even partial ones, we played Southwood 500. In this game, one person would start off as the batter and tossed the ball up and hit to the rest of the group. We each scored by catching the following:

- A fly ball—100 points
- On one bounce—75 points
- On two bounces—50 points
- On three or more—25 points
- Dead Ball (stopped)—0 points

When a person in the field accumulated 500 points or more it was their turn to bat. Also, if the batter accumulated three strikes (missed the ball three times) the person with the most points took over as batter and the batter went to the field.

This game was played at the old Southwood School lower field in South San Francisco, CA.. My cousins, the Morello Brothers—all five of them, developed this game because they loved to play baseball. Some of them still play softball to this day, some forty plus years later. This was a great way for kids to spend a summer day having fun.

— *Larry Jessup*
Millbrae, California

Sandlot Stories

Crack! Thump! Wack! Thud!

The pathetically ungraceful eight year old covered center field, considering his lack of coordination and his catching record of 0 for 50 he hoped and prayed that no one could hit it that far. The only reason he was in center field was because of his height advantage over the other players; he liked to think it was because he was a good outfielder though. Who was he kidding? With all that in mind his ego still wasn't clouded. Following the loss of the last little league game the team played, the friends and family accumulated over the season decided it would be fun to have players versus the parents.

The center fielder looked up at the blue sky in awe, he was surprised at the warmth of the summer day. Summer anywhere else means sun, warmth, blue skies, and sunglasses. In the usually damp rain forest of Juneau, Alaska it means blinding white skies, sporadic chances of rain, the absence of a visible sun, and long sleeves for anyone else but the Alaskans—t-shirts and jeans for natives. This warm day was a prominent one for a game of baseball. As the center fielder brings his vision back down from the skies, a new batter steps to the plate, it was a mother from the other team. A more than average sized women that looked like she knew what she was doing. From the looks of her it was almost obvious that if the meat of her bat met that poor ball, it would be a hurting unit.

Sandlot Stories

With a fresh count under her belt, she stood there waiting for her first pitch and he couldn't help but will the ball to stay in the diamond, "please don't come out here, please don't come out here." He liked to think he could play halfway decent, but he wasn't going to lie to himself. The leather glove on his left hand did no more than protect him from being introduced face to face with the ball. He looked up at the pitcher, his forearms resting on his bent knees, holding the universal stance of readiness in the game of baseball. His breath paused momentarily as the ball left the pitchers hand; it seemed to travel in slow motion to its home plate destination. His eyes the size of watermelons, as the thunderous crack from the bat inevitably sends the ball in his general direction. Even though it was more towards right field than center field, the chance of the little guy in right field catching the ball was slim to none and slim wasn't around.

As the wiry seventy pound center fielder ran over to catch the ball he was reminded of the fact that the only thing he's ever caught was that thrown at his glove, and a cold. In more desperation than anything else, he shot his glove into the air in hopes that it would land there. He must have resembled the statue of liberty; his eyes weren't even in the general direction of the ball, THUD! "Did I kick a rock?" He thought to himself. He was so worried about dropping it, that he didn't even realize it was already in his glove. Shock and awe slapped him in the face, as he realized that the previously airborne baseball made a safe landing in his glove for a change, rather than the usual THUMP, BOUNCE,

Sandlot Stories

BOUNCE. The onlookers and players praised the center fielder, little to their knowledge he didn't catch it on purpose but it sure looked as if he did.

• • •

Twelve years ago I was that pathetically ungraceful eight year old that caught his first pop fly in a game by accident. I played for another five years in little league. But playing with my friends in the Glacier Valley Elementary School baseball field tops all five of those years with ease.

It looked like a dust storm on the field of Glacier Valley Elementary School. The wind kicked up quite a bit, enough to blow loose debris and litter around with ease. On this summer afternoon the sky was blinding white again.. Usually my friends and I wouldn't play baseball on our summer break, but it occurred to us that we've never played baseball together before. So we gathered all the bats, all the gloves, and all the balls that we could find. My friend Jesse and I were the only two of us that have played organized baseball so we had all the stuff we needed.

We all met at my best friend Justin's house, at the time he was living across from the school. We all walked down the street joking around and telling stories about grade school. Walking next to the elementary school conjured up memories for all of us. CRUNCH! The rocks shifted under our feet as we made our way through the playground. "We never had this kind of equipment when we were in grade school!" One of us exclaimed. "Yeah I know, kids

Sandlot Stories

are spoiled now-a-days." We all replied. As the crunching proceeded under my feet, I found myself rhetorically asking, "Why would there be a large gravel ground in an elementary school playground?" We were all stumped. As we stepped through the chain linked fence, we realized that the dust tornados weren't that bad as long as we blinked often.

"Alright let's pick teams now." Justin hollers out. We had an odd number to play the game. We ended up having one person play left field and 3rd base, another person play right field and 1st base, a second baseman, a center fielder, and one pitcher. There were nine of us, four-on-four baseball with one pitcher. I picked up my leftover bat from my little league days, and stepped towards the plate. My favorite bat had broken at the batting cage. I took a couple practice swings, to see if I still knew how to swing a bat. After a few practice pitches, I stepped back up to the plate.

"Alright Joel, toss it over the plate this time!" His practice pitches landed about a foot in front of the plate. WHOOSH! Everyone in the outfield jumped. The swing sounded nice, I thought to myself as I fetched the baseball. After Joel received the ball back from me, I prepared myself for the next pitch. The batting basics ran through my head like a bad song. Legs shoulder width apart, knuckles together, point with your feet, all the tips I couldn't stand hearing now being told by myself. I studied the ball as it left his hand, CRACK! THUMP! WHACK! THUD! Laughter filled the field; I guess you could say we were that morbid group that laughed at each other's pain. We all hustled to the pitchers' mound where Joel peacefully laid on the dusty hill. "Hey

Sandlot Stories

you all right man? Joel—you ok?" I asked. It was hard not to laugh. It was like that moment in Americas Funniest Home Videos, where the blind folded son misses the piñata only to connect with his fathers pride and joy—we all know how much that had to hurt, but no one hesitated to laugh.

Less than two seconds after the bat hit the ball Joel was down, CRACK the bat pulverizes the ball, THUMP the ball bounces between the two of us, WHACK the ball ricochets off Joel's forehead, THUD Joel hits the mound. Now I don't mean Joel just falls to the ground, this is one of those classic falls where the knees didn't even bend before he hit the ground. That was the start of our uncoordinated game of baseball; we looked like decades of sports bloopers all in one game. We may not have been the most skilled group of friends to play the game of baseball, and yes, I admit that we were worse than we should have been, but play we did. On that breezy summer day where the dust storms looked worse than they actually were, I'm more than sure that none of us will forget our first and last sandlot game.

> — *Josh Miller,*
> *Juneau, Alaska*
> *Of The Tlingit Tribe Of*
> *Southeast Alaska*

Sandlot Stories

Sandlot Rules

My fondest memories of baseball are from my childhood growing up in a small town in Southern California. Yorba Linda in the 1960's still had orange groves within walking distance of my house. A neighbor down the street even had a few orange trees in their yard, a remnant of a once sprawling orchard. In the spring and summer months baseball was a favorite game of the kids in the neighborhood. We'd readily start up a game in someone's yard or even on the street of this quiet neighborhood.

The games usually involved about a half dozen kids of various ages which resulted in some interesting makeshift rules. We rotated everyone through batting based on age or sometimes name. If you weren't batting then you played defense in the field. You kept batting and running bases until you were out.

The thing I remember most though, was how we managed the age differences. There is a great difference in skill level between an eight-year-old and a four-year-old. To keep the younger players engaged we made special allowances. The younger kids were allowed more strikes, for example. Or they might be allowed to simply bat until they hit the ball. In addition, fielders stepped back at least two paces from their normal positions to give the smaller players a "head start".

These allowances were invented and agreed to by all of the players without any intervention from parents. Not all of

Sandlot Stories

the games went smoothly and occasionally there would be tears and bruised egos but overall the aim was for everyone to have fun and play baseball.

— Jeff Zandbergs

The Ball

The baseball-playing kids in our neighborhood in Pittsburgh, Pennsylvania were supposed to show up at the park at 10:00 AM on Saturdays—Sundays too, but one or two of the kids' parents insisted on church. So Saturday was the big day when we could maybe get eight guys together.

Eight would be perfect since that would leave one full-time pitcher and four on a side. It was better to have a full-time pitcher who could thow strikes, instead of lots of wild pitches and frustration.

I had a really good glove that I liked. I had it since third or fourth grade and it was broken-in right. Other kids would borrow it when they were out in the field, and I would watch them looking into it and popping their fist and listening to the sound. The only rule I had was that my glove could never be used for second base (or any base). I also had a bat that I liked. This one was at least a month old and it wasn't cracked yet, so I guess it was made out of some pretty good wood.

Baseballs were hard to come by though. The only one I had at home felt like it had dried out from being soaked. Or maybe a dog had got to it. I knew there was a better one at the park under some bushes, part way down the hill toward the stream. A couple nights earlier I saw the ball disappear into the woods in that direction when a couple guys were trying to play catch after it was really too dark to see much.

Sandlot Stories

We got through at least one and a half innings that day before my ball cracked open at a seam. I was playing first and second base when some one hit a good line drive that undid the seam when it skipped in the dirt past the shortstop. We tossed it around and judged it good enough to continue. Anyway, we didn't have much choice since this was our only ball for the moment. But we all knew that the game would be ending soon, because it's an insitinctive reaction among little-leagers to put an injured ball out of its misery as soon as possible. Now I knew there would be nothing but homerun swings until the ball was dead or lost.

I wanted to play a while longer so I ran into the woods to look for that other ball. I figured we'd need it soon. I remembered from the other night exaclty how it had sailed past the kid who had wrapped his arms around his head and ducked to protect himself from something he knew was coming but couldn't see. Two bounces in the grass, and it had vanished under a bush. No one had bothered to look for it, either from lack of energy or light.

It should have been easy to find. Two of my friends helped in looking for it. (My ball must have really started coming apart, I thought.) We didn't find a thing—no baseballs, no golfballs, nothing! There was nothing worth picking up. We thought maybe the ball was twenty feet further down the hill in the stream, but what good is a baseball after two days sitting under water? Anyway it was too slippery down there, so we jogged back up out of the bushes, back to the game.

Back at the game, I was amused at the condition of my ball. I remember throwing it, intently focused on the sound

Sandlot Stories

of the loose cover tearing through the wind. Not an obvious sound. I knew something was definately wrong with the ball without looking at it, like puffs of air gowing out of the ball as it spun. A good hard pitch lasted about three puffs before hearing the sound of the bat or the ping of the chain-link backstop.

One of those good pitches, a homerun swing, and a solid wooden crack, resulted in my ball turning into a big gray flopping rag, and a tan thing zipping into the outfield, and all of us laughing. The cover landed half-way toward third base. We all looked at it and passed it around before it was forgotten.

The thing that had started out as my ball was now a round hunk of unraveling string. After a few more batters, it was smacked into the outfield, with a long tail of string trailing it, and no one cared enough to even chase it. It was too pathetic. We left it out there in the grass, collected our bats and gloves, and headed home.

— Dave Parsons
Torrance, CA

• • •

Roberto Clemente, #21 for the Pittsburgh Pirates, was my favorite player. Probably because he seemed to be a modest player, who had talent and statistics to brag about, but didn't.

81

Sandlot Stories

Between The Vines

I love baseball. I've loved it ever since I could remember. Growing up in the San Francisco bay area, I watched Willie Mays and Jimmy Davenport battle the Dodgers and Maury Wills and Sandy Kofax on TV during the summer. I played little league, Babe Ruth League ball when I turned thirteen and even played on a winter league team in Hawaii when I was in my late twenty's. But no baseball experience is as memorable to me as playing ball with the guys in my neighborhood during the summer and after school in the vineyard located at the end of our street.

Since we did not have a playground nearby, the local vineyard provided the space for the ten or so guys on my block to play our version of the game. And what a game it was considering we played the game with home plate at a dead end barricade overlooking the vineyard with the pitching mound six feet below among the grape vines. Guys named Danny, Scooter, Kenny, Barry, Glen and Jeff along with a host of other neighborhood kids adjusted the rules of baseball to work in a vineyard!

Our town was Fremont, California, a growing suburban community located between San Jose and Oakland, whose claim to fame was the construction of a General Motors Assembly plant in the early 1960's. My family moved to Fremont in 1958, when I was six years old, just entering the first grade. My dad played baseball in Livermore, California

Sandlot Stories

in the 1920's and '30's, and even played some adult league ball when he returned from WWII, after a four-year stint with the Marines in the Pacific. He was a pitcher and played first base. He was tall, strong and had a curve ball that broke ten feet! He was a very good player. I know that from the stories my Uncle Joe would tell about how dominating my dad was as a high school pitcher. In fact, when I was fourteen years old and able to wear metal spikes in Babe Ruth league baseball, I found the last pair of spikes that my dad wore in an old box in the garage and I wore them for the whole season of 1966. That is a very special memory to me. I also got the sense from all the help he gave my brother and me teaching us how to pitch and catch and hit, that he really loved the game. I would venture to say that with all the baseball talk and stories he told as I was growing up, my dad probably wanted to take a shot at playing professional baseball in his younger years. But getting married, starting a family, and the war removed any chance of that happening.

The first game my dad took me to that I remember was a San Francisco Seals' game at Seal Stadium in San Francisco. That had to be in 1956 or 1957 because the Giants had not moved out from New York yet and the Seals were the only pro team that I knew about before the Giants moved in around 1959. The other baseball fan in my house besides my brother Joe was my mom. She also loved baseball. I can still remember sitting in the bleacher seats in Candlestick Park in 1968, next to my mom, eating our bag lunch, watching an afternoon game with the wind blowing in our faces. She would take me out of school once a year and we'd go to a

Sandlot Stories

game. I can still remember the smells of the stadium and see Willie Mays drifting back in center field, basket-catching a fly ball and tossing it back into the second baseman. Great memories!

Anyway, it is not clear who came up with "the rules" of how a group of guys could play baseball in a vineyard. The obvious problems are many. But we did it because nobody ever said we couldn't! We just wanted to play ball. We wanted to pitch, hit, run, catch and score runs. The ripening grapes and mature grape vines planted in endless rows with tilled soil that the farm hands kept meticulously plowed between rows, just made running under a fly ball a skill that would have challenged any major-leaguer. That was our sandlot! Nobody seemed to mind the obstacles much. We just made the most of what we had, and adjusted to the surroundings.

For instance, the batter was actually elevated above the rest of us, and we had to pitch up to him. But, he had to hit over the "end-of-the-street barricade" in order to get a hit into play and woe to the batter who topped one and smacked the ball into the barricade. The ricochets really hurt! But, we adjusted. The pitcher could not throw us his best stuff in the vineyard. It was a form of soft toss, but many a younger kid struck out when the big kids pitched. The base paths were also a unique situation. The batter, after launching one into the grapes, had to drop the bat, run around the barricade, down the hill into the vineyard and make it to first base before the fielder could grab the ball and get it to the first baseman ahead of him. The throws could be a challenge. Most of

Sandlot Stories

us were not yet much over five feet tall, if that. The vines, especially in the summer, were big, and the first baseman was not the easiest target to see much less hit. So there were a lot of guys reaching base. That extended the length of the innings but nobody much cared. We just loved being there, with all our friends, looking for our next time at bat.

A fly ball out was an adventure. Many flies were hit as you might imagine, especially by the bigger kids. But, maneuvering among the grape vines, trying to keep the ball's flight in view and not tripping over all the obstacles, kept batting averages very high in the vineyard. Some yelling at the fielder was normal when he missed a fly ball chance, but everybody knew how hard it was, really. We just hoped that the next fly ball went to the other guy.

I played there with my friends on the street for four years, and then we moved. I only came back to the vineyard once in a while, but the memories have never left me. In 1964, the vineyard disappeared. New houses appeared in the vineyard and our ball field passed into history. The boys grew up, moved away, joined the military, raised families; but we all still treasure the memories of growing up in Fremont, California and getting together for another game of baseball between the vines.

— By Ben

Our Uniforms

I played a lot of sandlot baseball as a kid growing up in Wabasha, Minnesota. As long as we had six to nine kids to form a team, we would all hop onto our bicycles and ride to the other side of town to play the "other" team. Wabasha's population was 2500 back then (and still is today), so the best mode of transportation for the road trips to the sandlots on the other side of town was always our bicycles. We carried our baseball bats with one hand, and hung our baseball gloves on the handlebars of our bicycles so we had one hand free to hang on and drive.

Playing sandlot baseball in a small Midwestern town, without umpires, gave all of us kids an opportunity to learn negotiating skills at a young age. We always had differences of opinion on who was too little to play, too old to play, and of course, whether or not the runners were safe or out at the plate. We worked it out between us. There were no umpires and no parents to make the calls.

Bases and home plate were usually pieces of cardboard. If the grass was too long, we used a jacket or sweatshirt or an extra baseball glove. There were no new baseball bats, of course. Most of the bats were the cracked or broken high school bats that were put back together with screws and wrapped with masking tape or electricians tape.

Our uniforms were our t-shirts, blue jeans, and PF Flyers sneakers. I don't recall any of us wearing baseball caps, and

Sandlot Stories

if we did it was most likely our dad's cap that was hanging in the garage ready to be worn the next time he mowed the lawn.

I also played a summer or two of Tball, then made it to the next level of Pee Wees. Although my PeeWee team was the Cubs, in my mind I was playing for the Minnesota Twins whenever I took the field. First base was my position, and I thought I was Harmon Killebrew. I felt proud wearing #3 on my jersey.

Our "road trips" took us to area towns including—Pepin, Wisconsin; Plainview and Lake City, Minnesota. I remember most the rides in the yellow school bus and playing games under the lights on the baseball diamonds that were tucked away in the corners of the high school football fields. Also, this was my first exposure to yelling and cheering parents encouraging their kids to "hit a home run" for the team.

I don't remember if I ever hit a home run for the team, or if we won more games than we lost. But all the other memories of playing baseball as a kid are like photographs that have been recorded in my mind for thirty-five years.

— Dean Plank "Pitssy"

• • •

I was called "Pittsy" after the Green Bay Packers famous running back at the time, Elijah Pitts. Jim Abbot started calling me "Pittsy" and it stuck with me through high school in Wabasha, Minnesota.

Sandlot Stories

• • •

I did not have just one favorite player. I liked all the Chicago Cubs of the 1966-1970 time period: Ron Santo, Billy Williams, Ernie Banks, Ken Holtzman, Randy Hundley, Glenn Beckert, Don Kessinger, Fergie Jenkins, Bill Stoneman. The LaCrosse Wisconsin television station broadcast their games in western Wisconsin and Southeastern Minnesota to viewers at the time. I remember watching their games on television on Saturdays and Sundays throughout the baseball season.

— "Pitssy"

Sandlot Stories

The Challenge

It was summer 1961.

For sure, there were no stadium lights beaming, no roaring crowd, and no freshly manicured grass. Definitely there was no Little League, organized baseball or even sandlot baseball here—nope, none of that kind of fancy stuff.

Forget about bleachers brimming with eager, excited and nervous parents, marked out bases, uniforms and the like. Heck,—even a tree for a landmark was way out of our "league".

The kinds of competitions we had were not even what you would call games. At best, they were just edgy, testosterone-driven contests between two stubborn neighbor boys. Here's a typical example.

It's a late afternoon on a sweltering hot, muggy August day on Juniper Street in our typically suburban neighborhood in Atwater—Central California; the early 1960's and summer vacation. I finish my frosty A&W root beer and shuffle off to Richard's house down towards the end of my street. We are two bored middle-class kids, Rowe and Covic, with nothing but time on our hands. You get the picture, right?

Oh sure, we fantasize about living in Malibu and being big-time macho surfer dudes, riding big waves and driving fast cars with reverb-soaked Dick Dale instrumentals blasting away on the eight-track.

In our far-fetched adolescent dreams, we are two buffed-

Sandlot Stories

out and deeply tanned studs—irresistible babe magnets with hordes of beautiful blonde surf bunnies waiting in line to rub our muscular backs with mineral oil. Our dreams are the stuff Beach Boy album covers are made of.

But, (back to our sad summer reality here) we settle for what we have and whatever excitement we can muster up on our own.

This is how pitiful it is. We have a ball. A ball! That's it. No bat, no diamond, nuthin'—just a ball. Our "playing field" isn't even a vacant lot. It is just the end of a cul-de-sac that borders onto a dumb sweet potato field.

Our "game" isn't really even a game. It is more of a challenge. Richard comes up with the deal and, as is usual with us, the rules are pretty sketchy. "Bob, I'll bet you a quarter you can't throw the ball from here down to the corner."

"You gotta be kiddin'," I laugh. "Gimme that ball, stand back and watch this!"

Now, this is a real nitty-gritty confrontation. It's going to have a winner and a loser. I don't plan to be the loser.

Willing to put my money where my mouth is, I announce: "Okay, Dude! Outta the way; here's goes." I take a deep breath of the soggy air, wind-up and then, with every ounce of strength I can muster, I let it rip. I see it rise. It's got momentum. It's powered to save my pride. And, there it goes—way, way past the asphalt corner and out into the middle of the old farmer's dirt field.

I did it! I knew I could. Now it's time for the pay-off. "Alright Rowe; pay-up, man."

Sandlot Stories

Richard starts laughing. Laughing! I can't believe it.

"What's so funny, buddy? Gimme my quarter." I look at Richard. His face telegraphs: "SUCKER!"

Not able to contain himself any longer 'ol Rick finally lays it on me . . . "the technicality." "I said 'to' the corner, not 'past' it," he cackles.

This is the last straw. I've heard this kind of thing once too often now. The tension mounts. I feel my face flaming in anger. "Get outta here! What's wrong with you Rowe; are you crazy?" I'm on the verge of going berserk. And then, in a surrealistic-type slow motion . . . everything comes to a screeching halt. Richard just jeers, turns around and walks back to his house. Is this how the "game" should end?

Fast forward to the next day around noon. Richard's hunched over edging the grass on his sidewalk. I walk up to him kind of casual-like. "To it, not past it, huh Dude?" He looks up. Bam! I throw the punch with everything I'm worth. A dead-on shot, right to the nose. I know it's his weak spot from our fistfights of the past. Just like Old Faithful Geyser! The blood squirts all over this white T-shirt. He drops the edger, I jump on him, we tussle a little but, basically, it's a done deal.

Now, our "game" is over. Sketchy though our rules are, one way or the other, we always play by the rules. This time the retroactive rule is: "If you don't pay-up, there's gonna be a payback!"

Oh, by the way, 'ol Rick and I have had a few other "disagreements" since then—but, guess what? That "game" was forty-two years ago now, and, we're still the best of

Sandlot Stories

friends! We just bet with paper money instead of quarters now.

— Bobby Covic
Incline Village, NV

Championship Of The Driveway

No baseball experience from my childhood matches the one-on-one whiffle ball games with my friend. It was a long series, dozens of games long over several summers. Every game was on the road for me, since every game was in his driveway. But he had the swimming pool!

Simple rules—past the pitcher a single, across the street a homer, no running (are you kidding?), ghost runners occupying the bags. Every fourth batter had to be a lefty, to limit the offense from getting out of hand. If your lefty swingers were on, you were in the driver's seat. The strike zone was tight, but consistent—a narrow vertical strip on the wooden garage door.

We had every pitch and pitching motion of our era down. Knuckler, palm ball, fork ball, slider, curve, screwball, you name it. Most were referred to by their foremost major league practitioner of the day. More than once did I go down looking on a "Marshall" bearing in on me from the outside.

Whiffle balls were kept in play until they were destroyed. Pitching had to be adaptable to the condition of the ball. A new ball did one thing, a flattened ball another, a ball with a flap of plastic hanging out something else entirely. Master the subtle differences, and you could be unhittable.

I don't remember how much I won or lost. It seemed like we both had up years and down years. I do remember it didn't matter at all. At the end of the game, we knew we were that

Sandlot Stories

much closer to the next game, and even closer to jumping in the pool. We didn't pretend we were Big-Leaguers, or in the World Series; we were playing for something bigger—the championship of the driveway.

When you're playing triple-headers, in 100 degree heat, on concrete, I guess spoke for our love of the game. I guess I still love it, since I spend most of my waking Spring and Summer hours on the Little League ball fields with my kids. Even without a swimming pool waiting.

— Pat McGuire

Fenway In My Front Yard

The landscape of Boston, Massachusetts has one striking feature visible only from the air. At first you might not recognize it, but the longer you peer out the window, the more you'll see of it and the more you'll see the big picture. Boston is positively littered with baseball fields. And as scores of them stream silently past—from manicured prep school fields to grubby and grassless dirt lots to the unforgettable Fenway Park—these peculiar green-and-brown freckles on the face of the city inform the uninitiated arriving at Logan Airport of what the residents already know in their bones. This is a baseball town.

I grew up in Melrose, a cheery suburb six or seven miles north of Boston Proper, which, for its size, contributes a decent number of those freckles. Melrose is a working class town that made good. Despite the modest single-family homes, duplexes and triplexes found in other Greater Boston towns—perhaps because of them—Melrose escaped the slow decay of urbanization endured by many of its neighbors. The commercial core is confined to one main street (appropriately named Main Street), and the rest of the place is residences, side streets, and lawns. These were my old stomping grounds.

By the mid-seventies, Melrose had developed a very nice and inclusive Little League program. Problem was, it ended when the school year did, and we kids were left to organize

Sandlot Stories

ourselves come summer. Playing baseball in the suburbs, however, is more difficult than it might seem. In the part of town where I grew up, the gentrified, rolling hills of what was once a series of apple orchards, there was very little open space. The entire area had long been subdivided, and there wasn't a single unimproved lot. True, there was a golf course nearby, but that's a generally dangerous place to play, although it's an exceptionally good place if you enjoy getting interrupted every fifteen minutes by a lecture from a foursome of old ladies.

Playing summer baseball is fraught with a number of other challenges. First, you have to get to a ball field. They may look like they're everywhere from the air, but it's a different story on your Huffy. And surely you will encounter a street that one of your posse has been forbidden to cross. Moreover, those fields are BIG. So it's difficult even getting enough players together to prevent you spending half your time retrieving balls that stopped rolling so long ago insects have begun inspecting them.

The biggest impediment to playing baseball, though, was our own backyards. Everybody had one, so our parents expected us to actually stay in them. "I don't want you going halfway across town to a park. Play your baseball game around here where I can see you." Of course once you got beyond the age of, say, six, and you were any good at all, trying to play baseball in a suburban backyard was like trying to change your clothes in a barrel. Still, we were resourceful. Teddy Roosevelt once said, "Do what you can, where you are, with what you have." And that philosophy

Sandlot Stories

is how whiffleball became the sport of choice on Sherwood Road.

Whiffleball has a number of distinct advantages over baseball, particularly if you're ten. For example, you can play whiffleball with as many players as you like (or have). You don't need a glove or a catcher. (In a pinch, you don't really even need a pitcher!) Nothing breaks and no one gets hurt when hit with a whiffleball. And the ball usually stops quickly after it hits the ground. Yet whiffleball never failed to offer us the best parts of baseball. The game retains all the drama and tension of the national pastime. Bases loaded, two outs, bottom of the ninth still carries all the majesty of Fenway, even if the batters box is five feet from your back door.

As I look back, I realize that whiffleball taught us the fundamentals that would help immeasurably in Little League and beyond. We learned bat speed and base running, and honed our eye-hand coordination. We learned how to throw accurately. And there's no better tool than a whiffleball for learning how to throw a curve. Thanks to whiffleball, I had the skills and confidence, at age 12, to pitch both a regular season no-hitter and a shutout in the Little League Championship. It was astonishing, later in life, how quickly those skills I learned as a boy came back. At my tenth high school reunion, someone started a pickup whiffleball game. Without a lick of practice in more than a decade, I hit the ball onto the (thankfully) sloped roof of our four-story high school a dozen times. And at age thirty-six and only 140 pounds, I have discovered that outfielders in my softball

Sandlot Stories

league frequently fail to give me much respect, often to their chagrin. Thank you, bat speed.

• • •

We always played in my front yard, because it had a number of features that made it highly conducive to whiffleball. To start, the house served as a backstop which, believe me, is an enormous luxury. More importantly, the yard had reasonable landmarks to use as bases. An ancient crabapple tree served as first base. We used one of those old, green storage mailboxes for second. A short, hapless bush at the end of the front walkway was the natural choice for third. (The bush on the opposite side of the walkway lived a carefree and robust life while its mate, mere three feet away, struggled to survive under the pressure of several whiffleball summers.) Home plate was a small patch of dirt in the grass near the back door, bordered on two sides by a right turn in the walkway. Every year, home plate got bigger, much to my Mom's frustration. She still teases me that it took her ten years to grow grass there after we outgrew whiffleball.

The best part about the lot, though, was that it was on the intersection of two lightly used streets, at the crest of a hill. Imagine a wide X across the top of a melon. The infield, in the bottom quadrant, was a natural diamond shape, while the outfield—the street—wrapped around it. Beyond the street were other people's yards, which served as the walls of our park. We generally didn't use right field because we rarely had enough players to cover that position. Fortunately, the phone company had generously provided us with an extremely convenient telephone pole near second base that we pressed into service as a foul pole. Only balls hit to the left of it were fair.

One of the great things about whiffleball, and pickup sports in general, is the existence of house rules. We had lots of them. Foremost, considering we didn't have a ton of players, was that you could put out a baserunner by hitting him with the ball so long as he wasn't safely ensconced on a base. If the play was a force, you could just hit the base itself. We used to say that the crabapple tree actually played first base for both teams. Also, to avoid constant bickering, there were no walks and only fouls and swinging strikes counted. Because there were no called strikes, you had to pitch at a reasonable speed in order to get anyone to swing.

Since right field was foul, all the playable fly balls went to left. It was a busy position. Once you crossed the street in left field you were in the Bleilers yard. The Bleilers were a sweet old couple that enjoyed the presence of young kids at play. If they didn't, our field would've suffered a serious setback, because balls were forever being hit into Mrs. Bleiler's bushes, which we'd frequently stomp in looking for them. If you hit one onto the roof of the Bleiler's single-story Ranch house, it was a homer. We declared that if anyone hit a ball over their roof it was an Automatic Grand Slam—four runs on top of the whatever was scored on the home run. Nobody had ever done that until someone's cousin, visiting from out of town, pulled it off. But he was fourteen, and after he went back home we decided that he didn't really

Sandlot Stories

hold that record because he was too old. Certainly no one our age had ever done it.

Without question, the best part of whiffleball was the fantasy. We imagined ourselves, as did countless boys across the country, as our favorite players executing big league highlight plays. My next-door neighbor, Arthur, was my constant whiffleball companion. Whenever he would field a ground ball, he would call out the play like a sportscaster, undoubtedly a specific sportscaster he'd recently heard. With a lilt in his voice, Arthur would announce, "The flip to Torrealba..." and underhand the ball off the apple tree for the putout. To this day, I don't know who Torrealba was (or, for sure, how to spell his name) nor can I say which team he played on, although I can definitively tell you it wasn't the Red Sox. Still, Arthur must've said it five-hundred times in the course of a certain summer. My parents still live next to his parents, and whenever my Dad sees Arthur, he calls out, "The flip to Torrealba!" to Arthur's continued embarrassment.

For my part, I was partial to Dwight Evans. In the '75 World Series, Evans made the best catch I've ever seen. Against Fenway's short, right field wall, he planted his feet on the warning track and arched his back, glove extended high over his head, caught a long fly ball, and somehow managed to not fall backward over the wall, thereby robbing the Cincinnati Reds of a home run. Even better, he had the presence of mind to double up the great Joe Morgan who, believing the ball had not been caught, had advanced around the bases. I had loved Fred Lynn all year, but when I saw

Sandlot Stories

Dewey do that, he became my idol. I spent the next two summers practicing diving catches and long extensions into Mrs. Bleiler's bushes.

And then there was Ben. The Fat Kid. I think every sandlot squad has a fat kid. We didn't like Ben a whole lot. First off, he was a couple of years younger than everybody else, and playing with younger kids wasn't exactly cool. Plus, he lacked charisma. It's not that Ben was a bad player; it's just that he always seemed to say the wrong thing at the wrong time, or make the crucial error that cost his team the game. On top of it all, he was just plain fat and ten year-olds are merciless. But Ben kept showing up to play, day after day, all summer long, plucky and optimistic that today would be different.

Ben's favorite player was George Scott, the Red Sox' first baseman-slash-DH for a while in the '70's. His nickname was Boomer which, of course, was morphed by Boston parlance into "Boomah" before the ink on his Sox contract was dry. Ben had chosen, not incidentally, a hero who matched his own proportions. Boomah was a power hitter, a fact that permanently enamored Ben, but as Boomah aged, his dimensions clearly became a liability on the base paths. My Dad once told a (perhaps apocryphal) story about how George Scott was so slow that he was the only player he'd ever seen hit a single to right field and get thrown out running to first. Boomah's velocity notwithstanding, he was a god to Ben. Some of the boys would tease Ben about his weight and disparage Boomah for also being fat (ultimately a tactical error, as few other guys would support someone

Sandlot Stories

running down any of the Red Sox), but Ben stood by his man. Ben would occasionally drift off into fantasy, swing his bat and call out, "Home Run, Boomaaah!" He did this at completely random and frequently inappropriate intervals, which would have pushed him further down the social totem pole had he not already been at the bottom.

• • •

I remember an endless day during the heat wave of '77 that must've seen ten games of whiffleball on our field. The evening was so hot that all the neighbors were outside and their kids had joined in what would be the day's final game. We must've had twelve kids in that game—even the girls were playing. It was well after dinner and slowly the parents assembled with their younger kids to socialize and watch. We had an audience!

Normally, whiffleball scores are very high, but with that many fielders, we had ourselves a regular pitcher's duel, and the outcome of the game seemed to hinge on every play. As fifteen or so people cheered the kids on, we played out the most momentous game of the summer, full of drama and emotion. Arthur threw someone out at the plate in the bottom of the ninth to stop the winning run. I made a sensational catch into Mrs. Bleiler's juniper bush, an act which elicited a huge gasp from the crowd as much for my fielding prowess as, I imagine, for the bush's well being. Still, I emerged, covered in prickers, beaming gloriously with pride, and holding the ball aloft like it would someday

Sandlot Stories

fetch a million dollars.

There were two outs and nobody on in the bottom of the tenth inning (The tenth inning! Whiffleball never went to extras!). With the daylight fading and his team trailing by a run, Ben stepped to the plate. I remember watching this at bat from left field, and though I was playing on the opposing team, I actually remember feeling a little sad for him. Ben rarely succeeded under pressure. With the game on the line, he was certain to fail in a spectacularly undignified way. I imagined him striking out in front of twenty-five people and injuring himself at the same time. Since Ben lived several blocks away, his mom would've had to drive over and get him while he took his pick of things to cry about.

Arthur was pitching harder than decorum allowed, but he couldn't help it. He smelled blood in the water. He wasn't going to lose, not to Ben, not under these conditions. Some of Ben's teammates began to complain, but he remained silent and stood firmly in the batter's box, determined not to look weak. Even I almost said something, and Arthur was my pitcher. Before the issue of unfair pitching could fully evolve, however, a small miracle occurred. Ben hit a towering shot to left field, twenty feet over my head. I instinctively moved back for it but I knew I had no play. The ball cleared the peak of the roof by an easy three feet and vanished into the Bleiler's backyard—an Automatic Grand Slam!

Ben trotted around the bases with all the dignity of a big-leaguer while his teammates went wild. The parents didn't know the rule and thought he had only tied the game. Some

Sandlot Stories

of the kids excitedly told them what this meant: that Ben had won the game and accomplished a feat worthy of a fourteen year-old. Everyone made a big deal about it, even Arthur. After a while, the glow of excitement began to dissipate as parents and kids said their goodnights and retired to their own homes.

Putting away the bats and balls, I remember seeing Ben head home down the lane that led over the hill. Every ten steps or so, he'd swing his whiffle bat and finish by dramatically extending the bat out in his left arm, striking a silhouette against the twilight. He'd freeze in this position for just a moment, as if admiring an invisible home run, and call out for no one but himself, "Home Run, Boomaaah!" Then he'd take another few steps and do it again. "Home Run, Boomaaah!" I watched him walk home this way, slowly sinking over the crest of the hill, his voice fading in the distance but still clear. "Home Run, Boomaaah…"

I stood at home plate, exquisitely weary from the heat and the long day of playing ball. I took in the sight of the yard, the street, the whole field in the fading light, while Ben, gone now from view, faintly serenaded the tableau. I felt fulfilled. And I remember being truly happy that I would get to wake up tomorrow and play this glorious game again.

— *Billy Griffin*

Everyone Plays

Yes, I like baseball a lot. I have been a baseball fan since I was young, since age twelve. I am a big fan of the San Francisco Giants and the Oakland Athletics. It is fun to go to Candlestick Park and Pac Bell Park and it is fun to see the upcoming superstars play and get their autographs.

I have also been supporting Little League for many years. I am so happy to see our young kids play baseball and the other sports—these kids are our future stars.

This year I had a great surprise. The President of the Little League and Vice Mayor of our town picked me to throw out the ceremonial first pitch. It was a joy to throw out that ceremonial first pitch at opening day. It was a pleasure and I was just so surprised.

I have been working with and supporting the Little League for many years and this has been a great joy in my life. I am proud to see our kids not only enjoy playing baseball but also get a chance to learn about being on a team and get the chance to play other teams. I think this is a really good experience for all of them. I help in whatever way I can and am happy to do this.

— Michael

Sandlot Stories

Michael Throws The Ceremonial First Pitch
For Little League Opening Day

The Thrill Of The Game

It's interesting how intense some memories can be. Some just seem to stand out from the fragments and blur as far more special and just far more worth remembering. When I was young I saw everything through a filtered haze of enchantment, often blissful, and also often intensely unique and sculpted to my own tricks of imagination. This odd filter has given many of my childhood memories a special glow and flavor, probably enhancing them beyond reality, but making them incredibly more valuable to me today. Now as an adult I often find myself so intrigued by my own peculiarities of remembrance. I cherish the poignancy of my own lens on the past.

I remember specifically my family's frequent attendance at baseball games. I don't really know what these trips meant for them, but for me, going to a game was definitely an overstuffed mixed bag of sharp sensations. The cold chill running laps around the stadium seats as the late innings ran long after nightfall. The distant roar and close mumble of one topic of conversation being carried across thousands of echoing voices. The cozy smell of peanut shells. Off in the distance, the field of people looked like an endless sheet of brightly colored tiny Lego bocks, smoothed over into row-long slots carved out of a giant cement slab. They vibrated and shook against each other with the same light plastic rustle, inspiring that same restless anticipation and adding to the definition of the roar.

Sitting there, soaking in the immensity of the scene, cloaked in my own thick drapes of five-year-old imagination, the actual purpose of the event usually was the last thing to gain full hold on my mind. The dynamics of the game, the runs, outs, scoring, and even the distinction between teams, they all breezed by my view just as excitingly as an errant fly ball, but also just as briefly. Watching the crowds around me, literally on the edge of their hard plastic seats, almost tumbling over down the steep section face, usually only made me feel a sense of vague confusion in the midst of the hustle and bustle. I never really grasped the source of their brief, if gripped intrigue, but the difference between us only added to the atmosphere of alien thrill that permeated my private experience of the game.

At the center of my secret little self-defined baseball universe was the immediate gratification of acquisition; an experience my small, developing mind could understand. And the ever present, all too eager vendors were above all the grand white knights of my private hunt for fulfillment. Every time they circled by I pleaded, begged, bargained and bartered the last drops of indulgence out of my parents for just one more. Moveable miniature figurines, gargantuan rubber foam hands, tiny plastic figurines, floppy felt pennants, and flimsy "punch-em" puppets, these were all the treasured jewels of my hoard of conquest. They, with their delicate hold on physical existence and a child's attention, defined the essence of "America's pastime" in my tiny scope. They were fleeting, engrossing, alluring, idealized, and utterly unattainable anywhere else.

Once my collection of precious physical attainments was safely secured, I would unfailingly migrate to rambling the endless hangar-like hallways on a hunt this time for the purchase of adventure and the revelation of mysteries, always with an obligatory guardian in tow. The cavernous cement passageways unique to the mountainous major league stadiums had a peculiar knack for making me feel very small. Their hollow, never-ending feel made my own youthful audacity shrink in comparison to the newfound height and stature the towering walls bestowed on my parents. With a finger safely hooked in a belt loop or nested in a large warm hand, I would cautiously brave my way around these more mysterious fields of stimulation. Up close, the faces of the undistinguishable sheet of fans rolled by my eyes like images from a dream, untraceable and indefinable but powerfully memorable and brilliant. And as the intensity of all the new sensations flooded the echoing stone canals and threatened to overwhelm my safe little fortress of imaginative fancy, it was always the reassurance of the familiar body heat of my now omnipotent parents, as I snuggled to their legs for safety, which took away the fear and replaced it with thrilling adventure. When they would then proceed to proffer up a long awaited box of sweet smelling Cracker Jack or an enormous, over-topped hot dog, it was then that baseball would truly become magic.

On the long car rides home, curled up under a jacket in the back seat, I would listen to the after-game play by play softly humming from the radio as my now tired out family

Sandlot Stories

sat in contented silence, and I would watch the glimmering haze of shiny red tail lights reflect through the window as we slowly inched out of the parking lot. In the calm of the warm darkness of the car, all the newness and vastness of the night of the game would slowly begin to melt away, leaving only a soft, comfortable peace. Like the residue of a Christmas Morning or a Fourth of July fireworks show, all the built up excitement slowly rolling off my quietly uncoiling nerve ends, eventually expanded and scattered into a tired out soft fulfillment that, in the days and years of childhood, would come to seamlessly blend into an endless golden haze of mingling treasured memories.

— Jeanne Tunney

Seventh Inning Stretch

The Hands Of Time

Growing up in the Bay Area of Northern California, I was fortunate to have two major league baseball teams within an hour of my home, the San Francisco Giants and the Oakland A's. To some locals, even to this day, a person can only be a fan of one or the other team, but never both. Some consider it sacrilege to even entertain the thought of rooting for both teams. But contrary to those who don't believe a person can like the Giants and the A's and growing up before inter-league play was even considered, the only dilemma that I had to worry about was both teams making it to the World Series at the same time. But I didn't have to worry about that until the earthquake shaken 1989 Series.

One of the best parts of developing my love of baseball in the Bay Area in the late 1960's to 1970's was that I had the likes of Mays, McCovey, Marichal, and Perry of the Giants to root for, and Jackson, Rudi, Fingers, and Hunter of the Swingin' A's. When those spring days turned into the dog-days of summer, I, along with many of my friends in my neighborhood, began my quest to emulate those players. In a time where orchards were being taken over by housing developments and the suburbian sprawl was taking over every piece of dirt, we were lucky enough to have a local elementary school as well as a church in our neighborhood to play at, on grass at that.

My best memories of sandlot ball come from developing

Sandlot Stories

our "over the line" game of whiffle ball on the church lawn. At times, it was just me and my brother and other times a whole grass full of kids. Whatever the case, it became a mainstay of my summers. Playing with a whiffle ball allowed even the most mediocre pitcher to throw devastating curves and sliders which added to the intrigue of our games and allowed us to imitate our heroes. The walking path traversing the church lawn in the outfield would often serve well as the home run marker, but at other times we would set up our bikes to create a fence. Of course the latter caused many heroic and later long tales of home run robbing catches and spectacular plays. We would often run our games late into the summer evening until we could barely make out the plastic ball against a darkened sky, but even then it could be no better than actually playing at Candlestick Park.

The church and it's lawn exists today, along with the scars from the bikes, and even now, I can still see myself playing a game that tests the hands of time—a game that I often still long for. Only today, I get to help instill those same memories for my nephews who are learning to live a passion for a game that still exists in the hearts of boys and the minds of men.

— Cliff

Sandlot Stories

Sandlot Ball Everyday

Growing up in Syracuse, New York was a mixed blessing as far as baseball goes. The comfortable summers were always far too short, and having a love of baseball meant having to cram a years worth of fun into those three months.

On the good side, we had the Syracuse Chiefs, the top farm club of the New York Yankees, and were able to watch such future stars are Thurman Munson and Ron Guidry pass through our team, as well as youngsters such as Fred Lynn, Jim Rice, Wade Boggs, Cal Ripken Jr., and Don Mattingly on their way up with the competing teams.

The down side of Syracuse summers was and still is, the seemingly perpetual rain, particularly to a kid inside with his glove and ball, waiting, watching, and hoping for it to stop, so he could run outside and play.

Myself and my closest friends never played a game of little league baseball. During summers we played sandlot ball everyday, all day, and often even into the dark. We honed our skills practicing and playing these days, and then by watching the Chiefs in the evenings. This constituted a perfect summer day; playing baseball during the day, followed by watching the farm team at night.

My friend Al and I would spend countless hours with each other, devising drills and contrived game situations, making the best of our two man team. A favorite was for one of us to throw ground balls, while the other played 1st base. Over

Sandlot Stories

and over, we threw hundreds of ground balls every day. This often took place in his driveway, which was not paved, making for a very uneven "field" with plenty of rocks and bad hops. But, there was one larger exposed rock which made for a perfect 1st base, and lots of trees overhead to provide some relief from the sun.

Other days we'd gather our mimimal equipment, and walk to Westcott Reservoir, maybe a mile from our homes. Here the huge grass field was like playing at Yankee Stadium, especially compared to Al's rocky driveway. We were able to hit fly balls to each other, as far as we wanted. Talk about a quick way to get in shape—playing the outfield by yourself!

This was great, provided we took frequent rests. I remember one night we had planned to do this the following day, but woke up to a torrential downpour. Rather than give in to the weather, we somehow talked our moms into letting us go. After all, there was no lightning. So for the better part of the day we hit each other fly balls in the pouring rain, drawing curious glances from cars riding by, but not really caring. A few of the balls we used literally had the covers torn off them from being hit while so wet, and the more intact ones were so heavy they felt like shot puts. We didn't care about any of this, allowing our love for playing baseball to be greater than any of these minor distractions.

From that point on, we played many times in the middle of the rain, which was really the best way to do it in Syracuse. We just made up our minds to play everyday. Waiting for perfect weather in Syracuse, might never happen, so we just

Sandlot Stories

played sandlot baseball everyday, raine or shine, and were the best all-weather two man team in town.

"Living" baseball as a kid, playing and watching in the summer, while dreaming and trading baseball cards in the winter, developed a lifelong passion for this great American sport. A huge part of watching the Syracuse Chiefs' games in the evenings involved getting to the ballpark as soon as the gates opened, generally one and a half hours before game time.

Since both Al and I were under the age of sixteen and each without a driver's license, much of our time was spent coaxing rides from our parents, neighbors, and in a desperate situation, even pulling together enough hard earned lawn cutting money to take a taxi. Of course each ride generated to the park also meant having to find another home, often at 10:30 or 11:00 at night.

Being at the park early allowed us to study the players' stance during batting practice, as well as fielding during infield practice. We became friends with an older gentleman who worked in the clubhouse, and so were able to enter what was usually a locked gate to the bleachers, and stand near the one door leading onto the field, through which all players on both teams would pass. This allowed us to talk with the players directly, and typically obtain any autographs desired. Very few players would turn down two young boys, standing by themselves, an hour before game time.

This routine of going to the ballpark continued through high school graduation, and even during the summers that I was home from college.

Sandlot Stories

It didn't take long, while trying to get autographs, to notice the language barrier with the players of Latin American descent, as very few spoke any English. Remembering these barriers in later years prompted me to take three years of Spanish in college, in an effort to communicate with the Latin players more easily.

All through college and then graduate school, the love of baseball and collecting autographs was consistent and strong. As a young adult, and by then a seasoned and established autograph collector, other fans began to send me their want lists of signatures they needed. Over time, many of the same names appeared over and over.

The idea came to me to contact these very tough signers directly, travel to them, and pay them for their time to sign a quantity of pieces, which I would then trade and sell to those who sought them. This turned out to be a huge boon for all involved—the players (most retired by then) were thrilled to be remembered and glad to pocket some extra money; the fans/collectors were excited to add an otherwise unobtainable signature to their collection, and were assured of its authenticty as I witnessed each one in person; and for my part I received a trip, and an opportunity to spend time with players whom I had watched and idolized in my youth. It was a win/win/win situation!

This recipe just kept growing and growing, and additionally I began to purchase vintage autograph collections and duplicates from other collectors. Over a two year period I made the gradual transition from my "real" job in the medical field to the "real" love of baseball and collecting.

Sandlot Stories

This all grew to the point about twelve years ago where it was able to become a full time enterprise/business, on which I've never looked back or had any regrets.

To date I've worked directly with over 400 players all over the U.S. and the world, locating some of the most elusive and difficult former players, and have amassed what is probably the largest inventory of baseball autographs in the world.

Every day at least one customer mentions their envy at what I do, and who could blame them . . . it's a dream to be able to spend each and every day talking baseball. I am really just a big kid who never grew up and in my own way, am still playing sandlot ball everyday!

> — *Bill Corcoran,*
> *Tampa, FL*

Sandlot Stories

Always Baseball!

Growing up we moved around a lot. I went to thirteen different grammar schools by time I was in sixth grade. There was just my younger brother and my Mom. My mother and father were divorced when I was four. Finally by fourth grade I found baseball and I decided I could do that because I could run faster than anybody else. This was in Los Altos where I was in boarding school.

So I just practiced every recess—every time I got a chance! All the kids wanted to play baseball and I got to be pretty good. Then we moved to Burlingame where all the kids had gone to school together since Kindergarten. I was the outcast. The one thing I could do well was run faster than anyone. In fact, all the way up to the eighth grade we had all these races and I could run fast. And of course I could hit the ball further than anyone. I hit it over the fence; so baseball gave me self-esteem and made me feel good about myself. I only had one really good friend in school. One reason she was my friend was because she was real tall and awkward and knew how I felt.

I was always chosen really quickly to be on someone's team because I played well. It was baseball, not softball, so there were always mixed teams of boys and girls. I never knew anything about softball until I started coaching my daughter's team. I mean it was real baseball! We never heard of softball. Always baseball, not softball, always!

Sandlot Stories

We always had races at the different schools, and I knew I could make myself run faster than anyone else by simply moving my legs as fast as I could. So I did! It didn't help me make a lot of friends since I was better than them, but it made me feel good that I could do something well. It was fun, I enjoyed it. I loved playing baseball too, I would play it anytime.

Thirteen schools to the sixth grade. We moved to Reno to the town of Sparks. I remember three different schools in those two years then we went to San Francisco—part of second grade there; moved to Burlingame for part of third grade, ended up in Los Altos—all over the place for school. Plus stops in Oakland, a couple of schools in Vallejo and places I don't even know where we lived. But, I just remember moving from school to school during childhood. It was really hard on my brother and I, when we came back from Nevada to California they put us a grade behind so that was embarrassing. I was the tallest kid in the class all the way through eighth grade. I was the tallest of the boys and girls.

My mother had made her living sewing and all of a sudden the WAR was on and there was no more sewing work. She had to find some kind of work. When we moved to Nevada she worked at a place called the Reno Casino during the day so she could be home with us at night and we could go to school. We were left on our own after school and she got home before dark. Which was perfectly natural. I would take the bus downtown from Sparks to Reno when I was just six or seven years old. I was a year older than my brother and we thought nothing of it. I met my aunt one time when she came from California and we went to a pancake house where we all ate and even my mother was there. It was like we had total freedom. We lived up to it. We were very good kids. I was always the bossy one with my brother—telling him what to do.

We always had to move around to where my mother could find work. Finally the war was over so we took the train back to Vallejo to stay with my aunt while my mother went to San Francisco to find a job. She got a job at Nellie Gaffney's, a prestigious women's shop on the square in San Francisco. They transferred her down to their little shop in Burlingame where she did alterations and fittings. At one time she made clothes and did alterations for Marilyn Monroe. Can you believe that! She also did work for some of the matrons in Hillsbourough. She made the robes for the priests to wear in Burlingame. She did all this when she wasn't at her other job. So I guess we were poor, but I didn't know it.

Oh, by the time I was in fourth grade I was in "love" with baseball—that was my favorite thing to do all the way through school. I would still be doing it if I were physically able to do so. I don't run anymore and my arm can't throw.

At the boarding school there were twenty-five children and we did play after school and at recess. But before we could do anything we had to do a lot of cleaning, vacuum the stairs, make the beds, then when we came home from classes, we would have to do our homework. After that we could go out and play. Cook would ring a bell and we would have to come in for dinner. We would just all get together on one of

125

Sandlot Stories

the fields at the boarding school; boys and girls. We never thought to separate boys and girls. We even played football together, but I was too rough for the boys, so they didn't want me to play. I never even heard of softball until my daughter signed up. I think it is a terrible game because it is just like those silly hats your daughter has to wear—make up "special" rules for girls—why separate? Softball! What are they trying to do? Make girls out to be whimps, because they are NOT! I really loved baseball, I still love it.

We went on a lot of "excursions" at boarding school: to the opera, the ballet, field trips to Mt. Hamilton, but never to a baseball game. We didn't have television back then and we didn't read newspapers. There were no radios or anything like that so we weren't in touch with baseball going on in other places. I never heard of actual "Teams" not until I was in high school.

COACHING: Years later as a mom in Palo Alto, my ten year old daughter wanted to get on a team. There were many teams, but there was a dire shortage of coaches, so my friend and I became the coaches for the Straw Hat Pizza team. It was SOFTBALL and I had to learn the *different* rules. We had a neighbor semi-pro come and hit ground balls and give the girls pep talks—he was very good. It was girl's softball, but fun. I ended up coaching for three years. I coached one year in Palo Alto and then two years in Fort Ord, California. My friend Sandy helped me coach in Palo Alto. It must have been 1977 when I started coaching. I really liked it in Palo Alto, but down in Ft. Ord some of the girls lived deprived lives, their parents didn't take them anywhere off post and

Sandlot Stories

they pretended to be real tough, trying to act older and wiser than they were. It was a little harder being their coach. A coach wants to improve the girls' attitude and self esteem as well as their playing skill.

I have always loved baseball because I could do it well! That's one of my best memories of childhood—***Baseball!***

— Gretta Adams
California

Sandlot Stories

Potluck In Hawaii

The Kaneohe Little League Program in Hawaii is where I learned to enjoy the game of baseball. Kaneohe is on the Windward side of the island of Oahu, where it is not too hot. There were many occasions when passing showers would sweep through the field during the game. I can still remember looking at the *makai* (ocean side) sky during the game and seeing the rain slowly approaching.

I am the oldest of three children. I have a brother two years younger who played in the Senior Little League World Series against Taiwan and another brother six years younger who played all the way through college. My father patiently taught me to keep score when I was eleven to keep me busy during my brothers' games, and I quickly grew to enjoy recording the smallest details of the game. I enjoyed baseball so much that I kept score for my brothers' Little League teams and our High School teams until I graduated. Since there was no Major League team in Hawaii, high school and college ball were big. I remember going to games at Aloha Stadium—the high school got to play games there and I sometimes took my youngest brother along to work as batboy while I kept score. Games at Aloha Stadium with the players' names being displayed on the big scoreboard were a big deal to me back then, but my fondest memories of the game were during the Little League years.

During the 1970's, Kaneohe was a community of young

Sandlot Stories

families, and the entire town fed a single Little League District (i.e., there were no competing baseball programs in town). This same League also fed into only one High School. Since Hawaii people typically do not move very often, the High School team consisted of parents and players that had been playing ball together for many years, in many cases since they were seven years old. So, these were not just baseball games, but were opportunities to get together with long time friends.

Every Saturday and Sunday during the springtime our family practically lived at the field. We arrived one hour before our game time and often hung out and played with kids from the other baseball families until the last game of the day, around six at night.

Little League in Kaneohe meant beer and FOOD. My children today get a drink and a light snack after their games, but I remember meals being served after my brothers' games. There were no "snack shacks" at Kaneohe Little League fields, so the parents brought food and made sure their teams were well fed. Parents in charge of snacks brought sandwiches for the boys. My mom would sometimes fry hamburgers at home and rush them to the field just before the end of the game, making sure they were hot. On other occasions she made fried chicken and *musubis* (rice balls). The fathers had their ice chest with beer and *pupus* (Hawaiian appetizers). Some favorite *pupus* were *Aku* or *Ahi poki* (*sashimi* with *ogo* seaweed) and *tako poki* (octopus and seaweed).

Best of all were the frequent potlucks throughout the

Sandlot Stories

season. After all the good food, this was a time for the kids to run and play till the sun went down. Potlucks kept the entire team and their families at the field for several hours. Hawaii people enjoy tasty (i.e., fattening) food. Everyone brought their favorite dishes and there was always PLENTY of food. We tease that at mainland potlucks we often run out of food, but not in Kaneohe. Sometimes parents would bring their *hibachi* (grill) and cook the food at the field. I can still imagine the sweet aroma of teri-beef in the air. I remember hearing coaches joke about selecting their teams based on the parents' potluck contributions.

At the end of the season, we had a weekend camp at a public beach, a park or a private beach house. Again there was plenty of fun, food, and beer. The kids swam and played all weekend. Water balloon fights were a favorite, and we would sometimes chill the water balloons in an ice chest before the fight.

When my brothers were selected to the All-Star Team it meant an extended potluck season and *lei* making session for the entire family. Anytime it was thought to be the team's last game, we made *leis*. If they kept winning, we kept sewing. When my brother played All-Stars on the mainland, I remember sewing *leis* and making coconut frond hats to ship to their games. These and other gifts (*omiyage*) were given to the opposing team at the plate before the game.

Through the Little League Program I not only learned to enjoy the game but also grew to love the families we played with. When I got married, several of these Little League families joined us for our wedding celebration. When I had

Sandlot Stories

children, I anxiously awaited the day when they would be old enough to participate in Little League.

We currently have three children playing this spring, and my husband has been helping to coach their teams since we started with the league eight years ago. There isn't any beer, potlucks, or camps, because we live on the mainland now. But we've met some great families and enjoy bumping into them in our community. Baseball has once again provided me with an opportunity to meet other families that have become our very close friends.

— Kathy

Everyone Had Nicknames

I grew up in Sparks, Nevada, East of Reno, which at that time was a very small community. I lived in a neighborhood that was primarily immigrant Italians and most of our parents worked for the railroads. We lived on a street that was paved. During the summer there was just a bunch of us that would gather in the street to put together baseball games. Initially when we started out we would scrounge up anything we could to play. Broomsticks to mops to whatever. Someone would find a baseball.

One of the neat things was that a few blocks down the street was a park and a Little League field. This park was called Burgess Field and is the site of the Sparks City Hall today. There were four fields within the park and they played Little League games there. Around the park were ranches. Every once in awhile foul balls would go in the ditches and they'd get lost and wouldn't be found. So we'd go scrounging around the next day in the water in the ditches with the snakes and other things and that's how we got our baseballs.

When we got that ball, we would use it forever. When they would start to unravel we wound electrician's tape around and around them so we could keep using them. One of the kids across the street—his dad worked for the power company, so we had access to electrician's tape—we would just borrow it out of the back of his truck.

Sandlot Stories

There'd be some kids that would come up with a bat—they'd get it as a gift. Or, we'd get broken bats from the ball field. Back in the 1950's the Little League would try to use those bats as long as possible also. But eventually, some of them just got too broken and they got tossed. We would get those bats and bring them back home, fix them with little nails and tape them up and we'd play with them. They got beat up pretty bad. We'd use anything we possibly could to keep that game going.

During the summer by eight o'clock in the morning we were out in the street. There was myself and a couple guys across the street; Buster and Billy were their names. Then there were a couple of kids that lived another block up the up the street, Mouse and Toad were their names and then we had The Hog. Everyone had nicknames. Mine was my Italian birth name, Corrado, for Conrad. My name is actually Paul Corrado, but everyone called me Corrado then. It was different, so that's what everyone called me.

Everyday we'd show up and we'd play in the street until someone had to go do something. We'd always be able to pick the game back up in the afternoon if we had to go inside. We'd play until someone got mad or got in trouble. We were only like eight, nine, or ten years old at that time. Our parents wouldn't allow us to go down to the ball field, three blocks away then, so we'd played in the street and we kept playing as long as we could—all day sometimes.

The girls didn't play baseball, but when we used to play on the street, we would ask my sister or her friends to help us retrieve the balls. We needed someone to shag balls. We

Sandlot Stories

usually only had one outfielder so when he missed the catch, the ball would just go and go down the street. If the batter missed it, he chased it and it made for a long at bat. So, my sister and her friends got involved and would help and run the balls down. Sometimes we would give them a chance to bat.

I had a friend Gino whose folks had a ranch on the Eastside of Sparks, but his grandma lived across the street from us. My friend Gino and I would play catch and my sister would help us. She got pretty good. We didn't have softball then so she didn't get to play, but she was pretty good, she could've played on a team. Once I hit her with the ball on her ankle and it swelled up like a balloon! It was huge and I caught heck from my mom, even though my sister was older!

Our bases were the gutters and the middle of the street was second base. If you hit one and it kept going down the street that was the homerun and we just kept running. There were windows on the sides and every once in awhile a stray ball would go into someone's window. That cost us some money. Most of the time the neighbors didn't bother us. We didn't slide though, on the street. We might have been Italian but we weren't that dumb!

Later, when we were eleven, twelve years old and older, we were allowed to go down to the ball field and play. Kids from all over Sparks would meet there because it was a small town of only 3000 or so people. Kids would show up and we'd start playing baseball. When we played at the ball field the girls never got involved with baseball there—it was just the boys.

Sandlot Stories

We'd have six guys against six guys and we would play for hours. Then we'd change teams. We used regular baseball rules for the most part. We didn't have balls and strikes per say that you would walk after four balls. We would bat until we got a hit. If a guy had fifteen pitches in an at bat, he could stay until he got a hit. Everybody got a chance to hit.

We knew who the good kids were and those who weren't as good, so we picked our teams to balance them. When we got enough guys on each side we would use, the "three strikes and you're out" rule, but we still never walked.

We would play until the Little League showed up around four PM and if they didn't show we had to go home soon for dinner.

I don't remember us ever getting into fights. It was a small town and we all just wanted to play ball. At the ball field if an argument did start, and we had them all the time, there were usually two big kids on either side that could stop it. Sometimes a kid would get their feelings hurt and go sit in the dugouts and then come back to play ball after awhile.

Another thing, we would take breaks and go over to the store across the street from Burgess Field, called Wright Way Grocery. When we weren't at the park playing ball, we were out scrounging pop bottles—knocking on doors asking for empty bottles or whatever. In those days you could cash in a pop bottle for a nickle or a couple cents. The guy at the store would take them from us and either give us money or just traded them for our food. Of course we usually bought junk food—those Hostess cupcakes or snowballs—those pink things with the white coconut on top. That was a big

Sandlot Stories

deal to save enough bottles to get one of those for a dime. If we didn't have the money we would still play ball all day and just get drinks at the fountains.

We collected baseball cards too, of course. On a really big day we'd have enough pop bottles to cash in and get food and baseball cards. We would trade cards like "I'll give you a Willie Mays and a Mickie Mantle, if you'll give me that Hank Aaron." There were a lot of us that had complete sets of cards. There were probably 600 cards in a set then and we would work to get complete sets. I had a couple of complete sets that I lost from them getting water on them in our basement. When my son was born, in 1976, I bought a bunch of Topps cards—ten years worth for him and I've been buying them for him ever since. There's some good cards in there—they are uncirculated.

We all tried to be like our favorite players. We would imitate them. So if you were Wes Covington of the Braves today, you had to play left field and hit left-handed. Or if you were Billy Bruton for the Braves, a bunt guy, you had to bunt. Or, "I'm Joe Adcock today" or "I'm Willie McCovey today" or "I'm so and so today." If you couldn't be like your player you looked stupid and everyone would make fun of you.

We were The Giants or The Braves or The Dodgers. We were more National League than American League. It was always the Dodgers, the Giants, the Braves, the Pirates or the Phillies. Once in awhile we were the Yankees because of Yogi Bera, Mantle, and Whitey Ford. There weren't so many teams back then, only sixteen teams, so it was easier

Sandlot Stories

to know all the players. The Dodgers and the Giants hadn't come out West so we didn't have any West Coast teams to emulate. The Giants and the Dodgers came out in 1958, so there weren't any teams out here yet. I was a Braves fan then because my first Little League team was The Braves. Hank Aaron and Eddie Mathews and that whole Braves team—I knew.

My dad was working and my mom would babysit for additional income. They weren't really involved with the baseball games, but we didn't really need parental supervision because we were locked into that street with all the neighbors around. We didn't really get in trouble. The biggest trouble we would get in was trying to get the ball or the bat.

Some of the parents were really great. We had one or two families that would take us everywhere we needed to go. They made sure we got to all the places we had to while the other parents were working. One was the Maldanado family. My good friend George and all the kids in his family were good athletes. They were the only Mexican family on the block. Mrs. Maldonado, Priscilla, was great. She not only supported all her boys in athletics, Ray, Jerry, and George, and later the younger ones, but all of us kids. She called me one of her kids. They had a van and they would haul us all over the place. That family was the only family that had Community Antennae back then. We had a couple stations, but they had six stations, one of which carried the Giants' games. When the Dodgers played, we would have fifteen kids packed into their house watching the games and

Sandlot Stories

Priscilla would cook tacos and fresh Mexican food and feed all of us. That was a really special event. Every kid in that section of town showed up for those games. It was a special treat!!

Priscilla was phenomenal the way she supported her boys and all of us. Later when I got into high school, Gino and I got into umpiring, and later George did also. The younger Maldonado kids were playing Little League then. Priscilla was at every game and boy if she didn't like some call—she would let me know. Once I had to stop the game and go over to her and tell her that I would forfeit the game to the other team if she did not stop. And she still told me what she thought and said, "Corrado, Corrado, what do you know!!"

I'm in a Rotisserie League now. There are a couple guys that I played high school ball with and some of those guys from our street. We have eleven members in this league, two judges, one attorney, three retired school administrators, a couple guys with a pizza chain, myself in insurance, and two guys in the medical profession. It's a fun bunch of guys. There's not one guy in this group who does not know who Priscilla Maldonado is. We all have a tremendous respect for what she did for us. Her kids came first and her kids were all of us.

We got to be pretty reputable as umpires. You talk about emulating people. Well, we would do umpires. We got into emulating those old time umpires with their chestures and they way they made the calls—Jocko Conlin, Al Barlack, we used to impersonate those guys. They all had their own personal strike three. We got really good at it. In fact, Gino

Sandlot Stories

and I were asked to ump the state championships, the Babe Ruth League championships because of our intensity to learn the game and learn to umpire. Then I went off to college and I got away from it.

I remember one kid; Buster was a good ball player. He could have had opportunity in baseball but he was killed in a car accident when he was eighteen. George actually got all the way to triple A with Cleveland with the Giants. He played with Duane Kuiper, who is now the announcer for the Giants, in Cleveland for a couple years.

Just the camaraderie that we had at the ball field is irreplaceable. To this day, forty-five years later, I still see those guys and we remember all those memories together and have been able to maintain those relationships all these years. It's amazing! And I've been gone from here for years at a time, twenty years, between the military and my job. George and I are both State Farm Agents today—he's down in Sparks and whenever we get together for meetings he still calls me Corrado and everyone looks at us wondering what that's all about. It stays in your mind all these years. I can still see us on that street chasing those balls down the gutters and watching those guys running around the bases.

That's all there was to do then, there were no distractions: soccer or piano, computers or TV. That's all we had to do—play baseball. Our parents couldn't afford to do all these things like kids do today, they were immigrants coming from Italy and they were working. So we played baseball—all day.
— *Paul Nannini, "Corrado"*
Sparks, Nevada

Sandlot Stories

• • •

My favorite player was Hank Aaron because he was so good...he was so good at everything he did. He was fun to watch. He did a lot of different things. He was a skinny little kid and could hit home runs and steal base and hit for average. Willie Mays could do it too, he got more media attention. Mickey Mantle was so good too and he was everybody's hero. I don't know maybe it's because I was a Braves fan, but there was something about Hank Aaron—he was cool, low key.

— *"Corrado"*

Sandlot Stories

Mommy The Coach

I was born in a small village in Kenya, East Africa in the 1960's. Kenya, being an ex-colony still had a lot of British influence. I remember playing my first game of "Rounders" when I was nine or ten years old. It was what we called a "street game." All the houses were behind high yard walls so no one from the street could see the houses and one could exit the house into the yard and through a gate that would open into a dirt street. There were houses on both sides of this dirt street where all the neighbors would come out to play in the "street games." This was a single lane dirt street where we had to watch out for lots of cows, goats, donkeys and all kinds of farm animals. As you can picture this was a very rural small town with one main street. It was a rarity to have a car pass through our road.

There were not very many people in this town. The schools were very small. We moved a lot with my parents all over Kenya—to every major town and city there. The sandlot or games we played on the streets took place in the little towns and not in the bigger cities. It was a very happy time—I tell my kids we used to run around the streets bare foot. We would just run out of the house—sometimes we did not stop to put our shoes on. Yes, those were happy times when we were carefree.

Looking back now, I realize that "Rounders" is pretty much like baseball. I had always just thought of it as one of

Sandlot Stories

our street games. Rounders is played with a bat, wooden or metal, and a leather covered ball pretty much like a baseball. We had four bases and a pitcher, who is called a bowler in Rounders, like in the game of Cricket. We were to hit the pitches thrown at us with the bat and if caught the batter was out. If the fielder fielded the ball and tagged the bag the batter was out. In Rounders, tag is called "stump the base" or "stump the bag." The runs are called Rounders from going round the bases and one scores when rounding all the bases in sequence. We would put down four bases and they were in a diamond shape and after hitting the ball we had to run to first, to second, and then to third base, which is so similar to today's game of baseball as we know it. There are three outs per inning and then the next team comes up to bat. Again it is similar to baseball because there are nine players on each side.

This was a common game for us when we were nine or ten years old and it was played on the streets and parks. There was no such thing as set fields for playing Rounders as there are for Little League in the USA. We would put down our bases in this dusty street, which were often just rocks. There was no formal field of any kind; we just created something when we wanted to play. It was just a group of neighborhood kids playing outside in the street, outside their doors. In some games, when we didn't even have a proper bat and ball, we used a wooden stick and tennis ball. Sometimes we would play the game of Rounders in school but this was never an organized game with umpires. We would have to make up our own fields with bases. There was never anything formal with Rounders in Kenya, but in England they have organized leagues. This was my first memory of playing a game that was similar to baseball. A lot of baseball scholars would say that baseball, as we know it today in America came from Rounders.

• • •

After several years in England and Germany, we came to America, about nine years ago when my kids were very young, and we started having them participate in organized sports: soccer, basketball, and baseball. We found that baseball was what my oldest son liked to play more than anything else. He played for four years before I took an interest in the game. I was never interested in the game that much, but we would just follow it routinely until he started playing minor league when he was league age—nine and ten. That's when it changed for me and I took an active interest in learning the game of baseball—maybe it was because his coach required the parents to take turns keeping score.

Obviously, in order to keep score I had to learn how the game was played. That's when I began my search to learn how to keep score—reading books and learning the rules of baseball. I even bought picture books to learn baseball. And as you know it is not easy and that year I believe I learned the game of baseball with my son, who up to that time was not interested. We both became die-hard San Francisco Giants' fans. That year we watched every single Giants' game that was televised together. My son, age nine, and

Sandlot Stories

I grew very close through learning the game of baseball together. I even bought a glove so that I could learn to play catch with him. The following year when he started to pitch I became his catcher. I got hurt a couple of times and gave up trying to be his catcher. I got the opportunity to help coach his team that year, which taught me there was more to the game of baseball that I still had to learn and understand. I do take him out to hit and we warm up together. I'm not that good, but I still enjoy trying. It is something we share as mother—son together. Baseball is our passion and now my younger son is getting into it.

Like you say, Silicon Valley is Silicon Valley! It keeps the people very busy. My husband works and he tries to take a role in the kid's lives, but one of us needed to take an active role. I decided to be there so my kids could have the experience of playing baseball, which they would not have had in England, where they were born or Africa. They did not have organized sport leagues in Kenya, only whatever sport that was available through schools. My boys would not have had the opportunity to play organized baseball in Africa or England. We came to the Bay Area because my husband's job brought us here and I'm so thrilled our children can get this opportunity to play baseball. I took on the role to be active and involved in their sports, and especially baseball because we love baseball and I could do it all year round.

My son now plays all year round and is on a traveling tournament team. It is something that we have both grown to love together, even to a level where we both have umpired

Sandlot Stories

games together! He is the plate umpire and I am the field umpire for the minor games in our Little League. We've had to do it at times when there were no other umpires available. That's a cool mother—son memory we have together. We both learned the rules and details so well.

Helping all the kids, besides just my son, is very special to me and one way that I can do this is by being the team mother. This is very important to me. My first active role as a team mother came when my son was in minors and had a very efficient manager who knew what he wanted from this team. In order to get the team together we had to mentor them and I had to mother them. The kids mean a lot to me and even more once I get to know them. It is important that I keep them happy, make sure everyone is taken care of and that everyone has something to drink during the games. I also try to keep the team together by making sure all the parents are on the same page and know where the games are and when the practices are. In Silicon Valley everyone is very busy and tend to forget schedules. I can't blame them, kids are doing ten different things outside of school, which keeps the parents very busy, and so I take on the role to actively make sure things happen—things like team snacks are very important to the kids. When my son was in the majors, I got very close to all the kids on the team with all the practices and activities. We've had good families with our teams, but somebody needs to be team mom, so that becomes my role—mom to everybody—make sure everybody is okay, they are healthy, there is a first aid kit, just that everything needed is there. I still follow the lives of the kids, I want

Sandlot Stories

to know how they are doing, and it is always good to know beyond baseball that they are doing well in their lives.

Before this, looking back, Rounders was just a game we played in the streets—there were no baselines, no base paths, these are fond memories because we played with kids who ranged from five to fifteen year olds. It did not matter what age, all the neighborhood kids came out. We made teams or picked teams from whoever was there. It didn't matter what their age was, there were no great players. Of course there were the big kids to look out for, but everyone was important then, everyone was part of the game…I miss that now.

It's different with the organized leagues where the kids are put on a team. They play on an organized team with proper bases, rules, and with umpires. Not having all this organization in our time, we ended up having fights out there in our Rounder games amongst ourselves, but in a fun way, it was a different sort of game.

All of this I never related to baseball until right now. Hey, now I realize I used to play something that my son plays and loves. I never tied it to Rounders! Today it came out, I've never even told my son about this. It's neat! It is something I've never even told my own kids. I never related it. I wonder why I never thought of this? Here it was all the time! I didn't play past the age of ten or eleven, then we moved into bigger cities, into bigger schools. There were no more Rounders' games, which were only played out in the rural areas as a street game. We never played it again, we never even heard of it again. It was so buried in me, that I never related it to baseball.

Sandlot Stories

One reason I did not relate Rounders to baseball, is that we never used mitts. Rounders uses a barehanded catch like Cricket—there are no gloves or mitts. The gloves were a tough one for me—it is not easy to catch a ball with a glove—I'm still learning

Being team mother today is more than just the playing of baseball, it a social meeting of all the people there. It's bigger than baseball for me, it's being a role model to all these kids. For these kids, even if this is an organized game, it is a social event where they make life long friendships. Many years later they will remember they were on a Little League team together. They will remember the fun they had, the games they lost, the games they won, the plays they made, the plays somebody else made, and this is all something that builds memories. I have built lots of memories, and for me it's all about these memories for my kids and myself. If I had my way, I don't think my kids would ever stop playing baseball, just for the social aspect. It's teaching me a lot and I'm hoping it's teaching all the kids a lot.

I found out that I do have a childhood tie to the game of baseball that I have come to love as an adult. I didn't realize until I did some research about Rounders. Did it really exist elsewhere or was it just something we made up on the streets? We Kenyans made it up on our streets outside and called it Rounders, but doing some research, I found there is an official game called Rounders—yes it is very old, yes it could be the beginnings of baseball as Americans know it today!

— By Manisha

149

Sandlot Stories

• • •

History Of The Game Of Rounders
From The National Rounders Association, U.K.

Rounders is played by boys and girls, men and women in every country, at different levels, from friendly games to international matches. It is a striking and fielding team game, which involves hitting a small, hard leather-cased ball with a round wooden or metal bat and then running around four bases or posts in order to score a rounder. Bowlers can bowl at over 60mph and batters can hit the ball at more than that. Rounders is supported by many local authority leisure service departments and has media support to various degrees from local newspapers and radio stations.

The game of Rounders has been played in England since Tudor Times, with the earliest reference being in 1744 in "A Little Pretty Pocketbook" where it is called baseball. This explains why the two games are similar and in fact many students of baseball accept that their sport is derived from Rounders. This is the name used by Jane Austen in "Northander Abbey." The "Boy's Own Book of 1828" devoted a chapter to Rounders and in 1889 the Liverpool team was formed.

A Dream

I think back to when I first moved to Lake Tahoe, and remember a very special dream I had that brought me there. Special, because somehow in my heart I feel it saved my son, who is now a man and on his way in his life. Before I moved there in March of 1991, I was beginning to worry about the way my son was headed. Not that he was doing anything that bad. There were subtle things, like the way he walked, and his attitude. His direction was not heading in a positive one, it was leaning toward some negative behavior. Picture this, you have these scales and they're tipping to the wrong side, and you try with all your might to tip them back. Well, it's not going to happen unless more weight is distributed evenly. The vision was weighing on my mind heavily.

My son came along when I was twenty-six years old and he had really turned my life around. He meant more to me then I could ever express in words. Let's just say there would be no words. It was probably not a real good reason to start a family. Yet it was the only one I had at the time. If you can, imagine the extreme desire I felt to give this son of mine a future, one he could reflect on and have happy memories of. I had a lot of really happy childhood memories that my family had helped to create for me. I've always felt that parents contribute in establishing those, and that some are good and some not so good. Memories! Mine are like a tune in my mind playing songs like, "Take Me Out to the

Sandlot Stories

Ball Game," "The Easter Parade," and "I'm Dreaming of a White Christmas."

I was born in New York City. We lived in the Bronx and it's a long time tradition there—baseball and the Yankee's. Strange really, that I would have these strong feelings, for I left New York for California at age five. It's true what they say—that the first years of your life are so important. You can really get strong desires at a young age that go with you through a whole life-time. Mine, like I said—baseball…oh how I loved the game! Everything about it gave me a warm feeling. They've always seemed regal to me—the Yankees! Three letters best describe them: "Wow!" I recently saw a cabbie on TV on the "Today Show," that had changed roles for the day with the host of the daily morning show, shed tears, as he stood on the field at Yankee stadium. He also was from the Bronx. The intense feelings that baseball evokes are evident, for so many people feel it the same way.

Now back to the dream…right before I left from San Diego to Tahoe, I had a dream. In the dream I'm watching a crate go off the mountain, and I look at the crate careening down the side, and I see tennis shoe's—a big size with the black and white high tops. And it hits me, they're my son's! Feeling terrified at the realization that they're his, I have no choice but to throw myself off the edge, and hope I hit land before the box does. In my mind I'm not worried of getting hurt, my only concern is to catch the crate, and shield it with my body, to serve as a cushion so he can be spared.

It was shortly after that dream that I moved to the beautiful Lake Tahoe area where my son got to play baseball. When

Sandlot Stories

he was a small child, I would take him to Kit Carson Park which is by San Diego. I would toss him the ball hoping to encourage him, towards playing the game. He didn't seem to like it though. Periodically we'd go again and toss the ball, but again it just didn't seem to impress him. I started to buy baseball cards and put them in a suitcase, and tell him some day these will be worth money. That also didn't receive any reaction from him. It seemed to me that he could care less. Only I wasn't about to give up yet.

Later, down the road, it came up again while driving to Tahoe crammed inside my 1986 mustang packed with my two kids, a TV, and our lovebird named Watch. I had bought a book on baseball cards that told what they're worth and the statistics on the players. I handed the book to my son who by now is showing some interest for he's trapped in a cramped car and has nothing better to do. Oh, and by the way, he was really interested after he found out that they were $$$$ valuable. I knew, that would peak his interest, what young boy doesn't like money?

I guess you could say that was the beginning to our new life that we were embarking on. After that trip in the car, he seemed to have a new fascination for baseball. All the way on that drive traveling along he would say things like, "Did you know?"…. And then he would give me more information about this player, and that one or how much this card was worth, and again that one. I believed he was getting into it at last. Once we arrived in Tahoe, we stayed for ten days at his Aunt's and Uncle's house. There he was showing his cards and book to his Uncle when his Uncle said, "Hey, they have

Sandlot Stories

a little league here. Are you interested in playing?" Clay said, sure he was. I smiled—at last he was going to play for real—not with mom who couldn't seem to get him truly interested, but with a team and young guys like himself. Part of my excitement came from my love for the game, and part came because my brother had always wanted to play, and didn't get to. This was really great.

There was something about the game it was just so real, so spiritual, like all the movies, I took my son to about the game: "The Natural," and "Field of Dreams"… if you build it they will come.. the cornfields, what a nice touch. Who would've thought it could happen like that? You know, I could see it—something just seems to click—the players coming back and all. I still smile when I think about it. It would really be exciting to have that occur. "Angels in the Outfield"—another one—see how it just has the magical spiritual aurora attached to it. I really knew it was the right move, when he started playing baseball at Preston Field.

His first team was the Braves. For my son and me that was special. Clay's grandpa, whom he was so close to, had passed away before we left to come to Tahoe. My dad was really involved with my son's life. My dad joined a church club called the Royal Rangers and he was the Commander of it. My son started out in the Braves in that club too. I really took it as a sign. I felt sure grandpa was watching and smiling down on us from up in heaven. I really missed my dad, and I knew how much he meant to my son. He was a "great" grandfather…but he was a best friend to him, and like a dad as well. Every time Clay played a game I felt like

Sandlot Stories

it was destiny. He was getting something very special out of the experience. That he probably wouldn't even realize—maybe for years to come.

At the games, I would sit in the back of my red pick-up truck and draw pictures of the field and dream about the Yankees and of course—someday my son would play for them. He really was a great little pitcher. Clay just seemed to get better and better till his next team and the next. Everyone loved the coach that Clay had then. Clay had him for about three of his different teams that he was on. That particular coach couldn't do enough for the kids, he always went above board for the enjoyment of the game. Thoughtfully, leading the kids in such an important time in their lives. My dad would've liked him. Everyone called him Silver. He might've had silver hair but was in great shape for having silver hair.

Clay unfortunately couldn't play ball in high school for his grades didn't cut the mustard. I couldn't take baseball away from him. He loved the game, so I let him play. Maybe I did the wrong thing by doing that but it made him so happy. Isn't that what life is about—finding something you love, something your good at. So he couldn't play in school. Really I knew he was smart and that somehow down the line he'd get the grades he needed. Not that I didn't advocate good grades. I just believe each child's set of circumstances is an individual case and should be judged accordingly. So I made the exception and he went to the All Stars game in Vegas, and had a ball,. He also got to play for the Babe Ruth League later on.

Sandlot Stories

It's once in a lifetime, and to me, his playing baseball was the groundwork to what lies ahead—making fine young men into great men, like Ruth and Gehrig, Mays… on and on… my favorite DiMaggio! This is not bad company, for a young boy to grow up around—like Silver, and all the many other stars. They are all stars you know. It's dreaming the dream that counts. Maybe they don't all get to play for the Yankees or the Giants, or any of the many other fabulous big league teams. But, the true joy and pleasure they get on the journey never becomes fully realized until much later when they become that fine man, down the road.

I've always felt the game symbolized the life we live. Like the bases, you run, to first, and then to second running running to win—just as in life. The crowds…shouting, and the teams at the end, line up and pass one another, slapping the good game—good sport slap. I really like that. That's one we should carry around in life and slap the good slap of approval more often. The game teaches so much, and gives and gives from one generation to the next. I can honestly say I love baseball and all that it brings to the field, for each young boy or girl gets so much.

— By: A fan for life…
who believes in listening to her dreams and the dream that playing baseball keeps taking you back to home base.
— Theresa Lacey

Clay Pitching
Preston Field, Incline Village, NV

Sandlot Stories

It Was The Summer Of '47

It was the summer of 1947 and my first hero was Joe D. (Joe DiMaggio). Of course the Yankees won the World Series that year and of course I went to the movies for Saturday matinees. People didn't have TV, so we relied upon the radio, movie newsreels, and the many daily newspapers for our news stuff. I remember the catch Gionfriddo made on DiMaggio in '47 and that DiMaggio kicked his foot in frustration because I saw it in the baseball reels in the movies.

The first time I saw TV was in 1949; one family I was friendly with on the block invited people to watch the final game against the Red Sox and Yankees. They had to win two out of three for the series. Of course it was black and white, but it was still a great thrill! Yankees won!

Growing up in the 1950's we had the three teams in New York. Except for a real odd ball on the block who followed the Red Sox, or some other guy on the block who followed the Cardinals, everyone else was either a Yankee, Dodger, or Giants' fan. The first thing I would pick up on Sunday was the sports' section because it had the stats and I really had to be up on my stats (New Yorkers knew baseball) to compare and argue who was better—Duke Snider, Willie Mays, or Mickey Mantle; before that, it was Joe DiMaggio or Ted Williams—that kind of thing. Baseball seemed to be everywhere you looked in New York.

Sandlot Stories

We had different kinds of ball games depending on how old you were. There was this elementary school across the street, it was like a middle school—right across the street from where I lived. As soon as the weather was all right, around early spring training or so, we would begin playing baseball.

In 1950 I played Punch Ball at around eleven years old. The older guys at school would play Stick Ball. The younger kids played Punch Ball. Punch Ball actually has two variations. In one, the batter holds a pink ball (Spalding Ball), and hits it with a clenched fist, then runs the bases. We played with as many kids as we could—sometimes with five on a side or nine on a side. In the other, the ball is pitched on one bounce, the batter waits for the right bounce and punches the ball and it is one bounce only, no second bounce allowed. We didn't call balls and strikes of course, but we waited until we got the right bounce.

When we got older we graduated to Stick Ball. All of us identified with major leaguers like Mantle, Berra, Rizzuto, Mays, Snider, and "Pee Wee" Reese; not to forget Bobby "The Shot Heard 'Round The World" Thomson. We imitated them while playing the game. My friends and I knew every name of every player in the majors and could recite the batting orders. Stick Ball was played with positions and there was always a pitcher there who would pitch it on one bounce and then the batter ran the bases. I remember going through the order—if the guy was a lefty, you would act it out and have to bat left. You basically identified the players of one of the three teams, Yankees, Dodgers, or Giants.

Sandlot Stories

Now there was another game played in the same schoolyard sometimes even at the same time, although there was a certain amount of interference. It was called Whiz Ball. This game was played with only two people in the game, one person pitched and one person batted and there was a certain distance the pitcher stood back. He pitched to the batter against the wall and there was a box on the wall. It was a strike zone chalked on the wall—normally a brick wall because it was the side of the school building. The chalked box represented the batting box, so if there weren't enough to play a Stick Ball game, you could play Whiz Ball because it always varied in numbers from a minimum of two to often three on a side. I don't ever remember more than four on a side and no one played beyond the fence.

There was a fence that wasn't too deep. If you hit the ball over that fence it was a double. If you hit it against the wall of the building across the street or if it went on the roof of the building across the street and was still retrievable—that was a homerun. Most balls were retrievable unless they hit a car. That was the tricky thing—there was traffic going on in the outfield and street cars. Even though there were no players out there in the traffic—we were all confined in the fenced in playing field—it was still part of our outfield.

The bat used in Stick Ball was traditionally some form of broomstick. We did not use the traditional baseball bat, but definitely broomsticks. It was called Stick Ball not baseball, so even if someone had a real bat, it still required using a stick. Willie Mays did the same thing in Harlem he used a broomstick, although he was literally playing in the street.

Sandlot Stories

We tried to get really strong ones and sometimes would find one tapered with really hard wood.

Stick Ball was a step up from Punch Ball and we typically did not use the pink ball like the one used in Punch Ball. The tradition was to get a "well" used tennis ball that had no fuzz on it. That was the ideal, not a new real fuzzy one. We would go to where they played tennis and find a real used one—these worked the best!

It was in those Whiz Ball games I particularly remember balls going in the street, rolling up the hill, down the hill and invariably going into the sewer and then having to be retrieved. We didn't come with a big supply of balls you know, so we had to get them back.

Sewers, especially in New York in the subway area or in the street car area, had round metal covers. To get the ball back we would lift the metal covering off, which wasn't that hard because they were so frequently opened and depending on how deep it was—maybe it was six feet down—someone would extend themselves down there by leaning over. Also we would use the stick as an extension of an arm with a wire coat hanger wound around it in a coil, a loop at the end, and literally "fish." There was always the "smell" to deal with when fishing down there for the ball—you really had to hold your breath. We would see rats and people always talked about alligators in the sewers which gave cause for caution. There were definitely rats down there, but there was also money. This was another handy aspect of the Stick Ball bat—we could retrieve the money in the sewer using chewing gum on the end of the stick.

Sandlot Stories

Depending on the logistics of where they are located, the sewer tops in the center of the street were used as a way of distancing for kids playing ball in the street. A sewer top could be a second base or a homeplate. If you hit the ball past a sewer it would be a triple and if you hit it past two sewers it was a homerun. The distance would establish what it was because we did not always run the bases. A sewer top might be the marked spot for a pitcher, infielder, outfielder, and a deep fielder.

There were many people who played Stick Ball in the street. We didn't have to, we were fortunate enough to have a playground. In New York the games were more likely to take place in the street, but this was Yonkers, a suburb of New York, we actually had a school yard. In the Bronx, it was the same, they had schoolyards and they were equipped the same with hard concrete surfaces. I remember having friends in the Bronx and them inviting me down there in their territory for Stick Ball games. Playing in either the street or schoolyards—it was always either asphalt or concrete….with fences, walls, and other obstacles around.

The kids ran the gamut of personalities. They picked sides according to who was there first. There are memories of a sign in list, the first eighteen guys got to play. In Stick Ball you had to have the equivalent of at least eight guys on each side or sixteen all together. You know—pitchers, infielders, outfielders. There was a certain fairness to it all—it was pickup ball and players were picked not by ability only, but by who was "physically" there. There were certainly players who were better than other players and there was

Sandlot Stories

age difference. There were actually leagues formed by the recreation director there during the summers. Little Stick Ball leagues that would draw from other neighborhoods, not just the people on my block.

I don't remember this in Stick Ball, but in Punch Ball there were some really good woman players. I associate the Punch Ball more with age eleven, after twelve or thirteen it became Stick Ball which I played right through jr. high school and into high school until I moved to a different area and played baseball on the high school team.

Scoring was very serious, especially in Whiz Ball you actually went through a batting order—here's Rizzuto, next guy in the order, now is Mantle or Maris. We identified absolutely with major leaguers at the Stick Ball level. There were sixteen teams in the majors then, not like today with all the divisions with numerous players. If you were really into baseball like every kid was, and even the girls got into it, you knew the name of every single player playing in the majors. When I look at my Bowman baseball cards from '50 and '51, I don't even have to look at the stats to remember who belonged to which team. There of course was trading of players, but no "Free Agency" then.

Another fond memory is when we took a break and the game was over, although we would more than likely play another double header or even triple header. The closest place to go for a soda was across the street from the schoolyard which was a gasoline station. In those days, there wasn't the refrigeration like there is now, so we had to get our Coca Cola, 7-UP, Pepsi, Orange Soda, or Royal

Sandlot Stories

Crown out of those big boxes that literally had ice in them to keep the drinks cold. It was a large container saying Coca Cola with a hatch that we opened. They were supplied with ice in it, like a big ice chest, and everyone went to the colder bottom to grab the one they wanted. It is a fond memory, relaxing, drinking the soda with the ball game on the radio on a hot summer day.

The games were always on the radio. A radio was a very big thing in those days. So with the three teams, we timed our breaks to listen to the ball game for awhile and then go back to the school yard to play ball. We played the regular nine innings and used chalk to keep track of the score on the concrete.

There was a wide assortment of characters in our games: we certainly knew everyone's name and of course there was a "Lefty." It was a neighborhood game, with kids from very mixed, middle class backgrounds. Yonkers in those days was like San Francisco where I live now, in a lot of ways. There were a strong number of Irish, Italian, Polish, and Jewish kids, but only a few African Americans and less Asians. Picturing my school ground is like picturing the North Beach Playground in San Francisco, where I played unlimited arc softball in the North Beach League in the late 1980's. Today many of these fond memories are relived and recalled in my present involvement of playing senior softball.

About sliding—not that we had to, but if we learned to slide we had a better chance. But we kind of had to learn how to slide on hard surfaces. We didn't wear kneepads or

Sandlot Stories

anything, so we sometimes ripped up our old clothes. We wore jeans or whatever and weren't afraid to get them ripped up if we had to slide.

Now it was kind of a short slide, actually like DiMaggio, he had a beautiful slide, where he quickly got up afterwards. That was probably because he played on those hard surfaces at North Beach Playground in San Francisco, where you just didn't hit the ground real hard. You kind of buffered it where you would get down and get up quickly and advance to the next base if they overthrew or something like that. But the idea was that it wasn't a hard slide. You could teach yourself to do it in that fashion.

Between Punch Ball and early Stick Ball ages, there was flipping the cards. That was done in another part of the school yard where there was a wall and we flipped cards from a certain distance. In 1950, I remember spending a certain amount of money, actually a lot of money in those days, on cards. In 1951, I decided I was only going to buy a couple of packs, a certain amount of cards, and win the rest. I really perfected my flipping! We had the match and no/match—there are books on this subject now. The one I remember in particular was much more a game of skill than chance. It was where we flipped a certain distance from the wall, the one that got the closest to the wall won. The grandest thing was when someone flipped a card that landed so that it leaned against the wall—that was like "double" pay. That definitely was a winner and we got a special bonus for that—like five or ten cards.

That's how I won my cards and made the natural progression

of "upgrading" cards. There was an emphasis at that time as well to complete sets of cards. They came out in increments. By the time the high numbers reached the West Coast it was already football season and everyone lost interest. Football cards were not that big then. High number cards never made it out to the West Coast. Only the East Coast Bowman and Topps baseball cards had these high-numbered cards, so this contributes to the rarity and scarcity. These were needed to complete the set. Most of us didn't care about doubles as much as completing the set we were collecting. A goal would be to complete the set without having ten Mickey Mantles. It was done by the buying, flipping, and of course trading taking place around that side of the playground across from the Stick Ball games. Kids brought their cards to flip and trade. Some actually did put them in the spokes of their bicycles, which made an interesting sound while riding. Card collecting was an avid hobby until my teenage years when I discovered girls.

Parents—The days are longer in the summer, so right after school we got into our play clothes. We didn't wear uniforms, but there were baseball hats that we would often wear. Around dinner time we would take a break to have dinner. Dad was home from work, I would see him, and than I would go back to the school yard. Late in the evening, say 8:00 or 7:30 PM, parents would come down to what was called the "stoop" area around the apartment buildings. They would bring the equivalent of folding chairs, both men and women, and they would be playing card games outside. They played games like Pinochle, Pocker, Gin Rummy, or

Sandlot Stories

Canasta while listening to the ball game on a radio. They had their own little thing of getting together. The main thing for them also was being able to get out of the apartment in the summer because nights were very, very hot. There was no air-conditioning and very few fans. They would sit outside in these fold up chairs, outside of their particular apartment, playing cards, talking or listening to the game. When transistor radios came out, that was a big thing—to be able to sit outside and listen to the Yankees, Dodgers, or Giants.

Also around that time I remember going to "the country," that is something my parents would do every year. We got out of New York in the summer when it was too hot. Even in "the country" we played morning softball games with the people staying at the hotel—adults and kids, but mostly the adults. Fortunately, I often got to play.

• • •

After moving to San Francisco in 1976, I began going to local card and sports memorabilia shows. In 1978 just after the "Reggie Bars" arrived I decided once again to collect a particular player rather than sets of cards. I chose Reggie Jackson to collect since I had always been and continue to be a Yankee fan and Reggie was with the Yankees at that time. It now has been over twenty-five continuous years of collecting Reggie cards and memorabilia. In 2001 I essentially retired from being an architect and today continue to play Senior Softball and collect while meeting some great people along the way. Almost like the Summer of '47.

Sandlot Stories

● ● ●

When my mother was in her eighty's my father had already died. My wife and I were living in San Francisco at the time when we went to visit her in a secluded area north of Yonkers. It wasn't going to be a pleasant trip for me because she was forgetting things and she was old. We rented a car from La Guardia Airport and drove past the Bronx and past Yankee Stadium, which was all lit up. The ball game was on, so I turned on the radio.

We parked and walked up the stairs to take the elevator to a special floor, which was a kind of assisted-care nursing area. It was a hot night and all the doors were open to every room. As we walked down the hall with linoleum floors and institutional walls to see my elderly mother, we passed the rooms of other older women needing the same kind of care. It would have been depressing except for the TV's and radios heard from each room—nine out of ten of these women had the baseball game on!

From their beds or wheel-chairs they were watching or listening to that game in the same way they had for years with their husbands and friends. Some of those women were very knowledgeable and others used it simply as background noise that reminded them of their husbands and those times like when I was a kid and they were young. I'm sure of this…This chilled me and made the back of my hair stand up. Again, it wasn't a pleasant experience going to see my

Sandlot Stories

mother this way. Hearing the game on in all those rooms, even if they were not looking at the TV's but just using it as background noise, was heart rending.

We got used to the honking in New York—it was part of our life. I live in San Francisco now and have two freeways that sound like the ocean to me except for an occasional siren. The background sounds of New York, on a hot summer evening like this, were the honking in the street, the streetcars, and baseball on the radio. To these older, New York women, *the sound of baseball was the sound of life.*

— Allen Statler
San Francisco

The Game That Never Ends

Our Home Plate

Under every high tech company in Silicon Valley, California, there once was an orchard, home to a childhood baseball field. Even under the lawn of a large Church, I still recognize the home plate of my baseball field.

Saratoga was a small town in the 1950's that would later become home to many Silicon Valley high tech entrepreneurs. Growing up in the 1960's and 1970's Saratoga was anything but high tech. Instead its mark was one of fruit orchards, like the rest of what was to become Silicon Valley. Downtown Saratoga, known as Saratoga Village, had as its Main Street, Big Basin Way. This consisted of a grocery store, Chrislows, where Mom would buy our clothes, a hardware store where the guys hung out, the Plumed Horse Restaurant, a post office, and a little fire station on the corner. The Plumed Horse Restaurant, started in the 1950's from what had been originally a stable, was reserved for special occasions and still a place I frequent today with business guests from Japan.

For my friends, summer jobs in Saratoga consisted of newspaper routes and picking apricots. Apricot picking gave an added bonus that included opportunities to perfect the accuracy of our throwing arms with apricot fights and distance contests during our breaks. The few cents we made would quickly be exchanged for baseball cards as we rode our bicycles through the orchard shortcut, past the little

Sandlot Stories

Swim Club to the grocery store. We would put our nickle in the slot and turn the silver knob of the red baseball card/gumball machine that sat outside the grocery store. This machine always showed five cards pasted on cardboard and of course they would be superstar players like Mickey Mantle, Roberto Clemente, Willie Mays, etc. Each time I anxiously anticipated the five cards that would come from my nickle, hoping for a superstar or at least a San Francisco Giants' player. For the next four years we would feed our coins into the same red baseball card machine, always hoping for the "big one."

The payoff came in 1967 for my best friend Steve, when he put in three nickles and came up with all Willie Mays' cards. I wasn't there to see this machine finally pay off, but everytime I think of baseball cards, I picture those pristine 1967 baseball cards with the blue sky background and the bold green lettering at the bottom of the card spelling "GIANTS" and the headshot of Willie Mays smiling. Then I think of that little red gumball machine that sat in front of the grocery store.

But most of all, summers for Steve and I revolved around playing baseball. Springing up all around Saratoga were new houses, with new kids, as the orchards were disappearing. I was the luckiest of all my friends, when the largest lot in our neighborhood was saved. No, not for a baseball field, but it could have been. The lot was saved for a large church, which wouldn't be completed for a year. During that year, on that hallowed ground, I learned the game of baseball with Steve and my younger brother.

Sandlot Stories

When the church was finished, we watched a beautiful manicured lawn cover the back part of the lot and realized an even bigger treasure. In our minds, the lawn growing within a roped off area was being staked out for our new baseball field. Coming home one afternoon, seeing that the stakes and the cord around the lawn were gone, was just like having braces come off your teeth and thinking of all the new things you could now eat.

The corner of the lawn had been earmarked as home plate and was eventually worn into a permanent brown spot, even with Mom sprinkling grass seed at night after we were asleep. First base was a small tree that lined the right side of the field. Second base was the pine tree straight ahead. For third base, a shirt always marked the spot. A home run was over the black asphalt sidewalk leading up to the church. Each day, the priest would stop on the sidewalk to watch, as if disbelieving we could hit a ball that far. But, with each new summer we came closer, until we could hit past the sidewalk. My friend Brian hit the farthest!

It was his hit that made us realize we were no longer those little boys who were the first to mark this field. One day, he hit the white roof of the oval church. We considered ourselves lucky that it wasn't a window. Even without a broken window, it must have sounded pretty awful inside that domed Church the way everyone came running out!

Later as an adult, I still recognized that permanent brown spot on the lawn as home plate and the surroundings as my childhood baseball field. I'm sure most people driving past the church wondered why there was a brown spot on this

Sandlot Stories

meticulously maintained lawn. Long after we left, a second generation of kids used our spot as home plate.

It took years for the grass to grow over that little brown spot, but underneath that grass will always be *our* home plate.

> — *"The Little Warrior*
> — #7

· · ·

Yes, I was a little warrior who relentlessly practiced and perfected the fundamental baseball principles each time I went out. Whether the kids were bigger or older didn't seem to matter, I was determined to "play." Clothed in my best jeans—the ones with the holes in the knees and the permanent grass stains, my white "T" shirt with a number "7" marked on the back with a grease pen, my black PF Flyer tennis shoes, a cracked wooden bat in hand, and a well used Wilson, "Ron Perranoski" model glove hanging from my bat, I was a "little warrior" headed to battle. When I returned from the field with new holes from sliding, new grass stains from diving for catches, and a healthy dusting of dirt from avoiding brush back pitches everyone remarked, "Is this how you play baseball?"—Oh yeah!

Sandlot Stories

Our Home Plate

When the Game is Over ...

With each new season, from sandlot through organized ball, my passion for the game grew. How long will these moments last? I was tempted with talent to play beyond childhood, but never with thoughts that it would one day pass. The clues were there: some hit further and others threw harder, but my dream remained. Suddenly, one summer, the game ended. Mom was right; it wasn't bad to have gone to college at night. It wasn't bad to study business, along with perfecting a curve ball. It was time to put away, both bat and glove for a "real" job—when the game was over!

Spring came again, but it would be inside a defense company. A city within a city; windowless buildings, ID badges, time clocks and timed lunches—a far cry from my endless days on baseball fields, under blue-sky with mountain backdrops. From staring down batters, I was now staring at computer screens.

As summer rolled into full swing, baseball entered my life again. I'm not sure how it happened—at a water fountain or waiting in a cafeteria line. I was "challenged" to a softball game. Faced with no team and challenged by one of the company's best ("A" teams), along came my friend Bill, who daily mentored my work skills, to join my cause. Bill, no stranger to baseball, had just managed in the Little League World Series.

With Bill in hand, a company team was formed: Butch at

Sandlot Stories

catcher, Joe at first, Eddie at second, Roger at short, Kevin at third, and the outfield of Tom, Joe, and myself. With Bill taking care of pitching and Lisa taking care of snacks and drinks, we looked like a "sand!ot" or "baseball happy hour" team, which was incentive for some to play. With all shapes and sizes, and ages, from twenty to fifty, we took that field.

As 6:00 PM approached, on Friday afternoon, across the parking lot came our challengers, swaggering in matching uniforms. While perfectly tuned and swinging powerful bats, stretching and snapping the ball, back and forth in unison, our "sandlot" team watched in awe. Having never played together as a team, we quickly found ourselves on the short side of the score.

For those who thought it would be easy, like myself, hitting a grapefruit size ball, tossed like an egg, resulted in nothing more than deep fly balls. In the field, the challengers found our holes, with "placed" line drives. The first three innings became a "baseball happy hour" with our team enduring ribs and pokes that went along with the score. But somewhere around the fourth, snacks and drinks took a back seat, to playing this game for "sandlot pride!"

In the last two, we no longer played like the "sandlot" team that started at 6:00. As darkness rolled in, with another inning to go, the challengers called the game. With our ragtag team one run short, the elite claimed they did not want to get hurt in the encroaching darkness. It was face saving, with all of us knowing that if the game hadn't been called, the ending would have been different.

As we left the field for pizza, some of us were asked to join

Sandlot Stories

the elite team, others went back to playing on coed teams, and others just went back to their jobs.

But we all knew, when the game was over . . . there would never be a rematch!

— #7

First Pick?

The movie "Top Gun" and the song, "No Points For Second Best," could sometimes summarize my simple sandlot games. Of the many ball games I played, one would change my life. Till that game, my life had been about winning—no points for second best. But all along under "my home plate" long after "the game was over…" I found out what life was really all about.

While choosing sides for a pickup game, I was directed to a boy standing alone in the outfield. Alongside me, another boy whispered, "That's the one you want to pick first." "Alone In The Outfield" had a right-handed glove jammed on his "right hand" and was walking the ball back into the infield after every hit. He was everything that I would not have picked first. It wouldn't have taken a rocket scientist to figure out he was not the best player on the field that day, let alone any day. "You've got to be kidding?" I said. But my friend was not kidding; he knew something I had yet to learn. We all know someone like this: the one who never gets to play, the one that never measures up, or the one nobody wants.

"Alone In The Outfield" was not my first pick, but when that sandlot game ended, it was a game I would never forget for the rest of my life. I picked "Alone In The Outfield" first. You should have seen the look on his face—as if he was saying, "First, me? You want me?" What does it matter that

Sandlot Stories

"Alone In The Outfield" never became a baseball star; what does it matter if we won or lost the game. He will always remember he was first pick and I will always remember the look on his face!

On *my home plate*, long after the cheers are gone, that game will always be number one. It wasn't about winning that day, but it was about how I played the game—thanks Ben.

— #7

Sandlot Stories

The Shadow or the Ball?

The Sandlot

Only in the beauty of Creation
A disorgainzed organization
The music of fun
The colors - the glee of pure excitement
We all can win

I was always afraid of baseball; afraid I would get hit right in the head by the ball, afraid of the shadow of the ball, actually. I wore glasses, so with the sun shining into my eyes in the outfield on a warm Southern California day, I was never sure which one was the real McCoy—the ball or its shadow.

You see, I was a shy and uncoordinated little girl who thought that baseball was ridiculous. The fanciful running around in a circle, pushing oneself beyond one's limits seemed like a useless exercise in the human ego. How could anyone be better than anyone else? No one ever asked me to play. I was like Janis Ian at "Seventeen" only I learned it at an earlier age.

One day at recess a group of us sort of fell into a sandlot game, if it were to have a name. I guess we didn't choose

Sandlot Stories

sides. I was the first to go up hoping to bat. I did not expect to be picked because I was shy, insecure, scared and didn't think I fit in or would be able to even play ball. One of the so-called "trouble makers" told me, "It's your turn!" I was honored, but frozen. They yelled at me, "Go girl! Go!"

So one of the troublemakers, just one day, out of the goodness of her heart and for no apparent reason, picked me! My throat went raw like a cold cucumber. I wanted to cry.

But she yelled, "You can do it! Go girl! Go!"

My body was shaking with excitement. My one and only chance to prove I was something to these people had arrived. Then she yelled, "Pretend it's _____!" —that Vice Principle we were all in fear of.

"I can do this," I thought. There he was, that Vice Principle in front of me, glaring at me, glaring at all of the trouble makers including my new friend. I wonder if all the hard-headed principles, vice principles, counselors, and other administrators in my life were put there merely to jerk me around or did they teach me how to hit the ball? My meager ego clashing with theirs, "I'll show him!" "You'll see!" "I'll show her!"

In all my life, from as far back as I can remember, I was made fun of, but God was always there. I could tell you dozens of times that He came through for me. So many times He appeared on my doorstep just when I needed Him. Do Angels speak through others? I heard it from within me . . . "You can do this. Focus. You've got it in you. Here comes the ball." Something rose up in me and the ball became them all—WHAM!

Sandlot Stories

Suddenly everyone was yelling and I was running. The outfielder dropping the ball and the others falling all over each other to get it. Suddenly I was a baseball star!

It happened more than once from that day forward—my heart in a rhythm with my soul, on to completion, pushing myself beyond my means, running around in a circle—safely to home base. Was this what one felt like when in tune with the universe and with God?

There have been other moments of pure exhilaration since that time—so many "Sandlot Games"—a multitude of human hurdles and mountains to climb.

Today I can thank all the boogie men in my life; the antangonizers; the intimidators, the low-lifes . . . Angels in a way that lead me to a higher place.

— Melinda Potter
Tahoe Vista, CA

185

Sandlot Stories

Play Ball!

Growing up in the Dobbins' household was never boring. My memories of baseball are mostly memories of bonding with my father; which is not such a bad thing. There are many stories to tell about my Dad. We played catch on the front lawn every day for hours on end. He helped coach my Little League games and was always interested in any sport I played. When I witnessed the final professional baseball game at Candlestick Park I realized that along with Dad, that we had seen roughly a thousand games there over the thirty-nine years he and I were together.

Our story is more than the actual viewing of a game. The act of going to a game was surrounded by something much more awe inspiring as a child—the hunt for an autograph. Today, the use of the word "hunt" would mean something different, since collecting is a big business. But for me, as a child in the 1960's, it meant the excitement I felt in trying to get another player's autograph.

In those days, players were honored to grant an autograph. Most would sign as many things for you as you had, but there was etiquette to this ritual and it was considered rude to ask for more than two or three at the absolute most. Lesson number one that I learned from my father was to respect each person's privacy. We weren't trying to "get something out of them." The thought of reselling an autograph and not putting this newly prized possession directly into your

Sandlot Stories

collection was beyond our wildest dream. The thought of a player charging money for his autograph was truly a distant nightmare.

The night before going to a game was as involved as homework. But this was the fun kind of homework. My father and I would sit down on the floor; I would usually have the team roster from the newspaper and begin to sort out what cards and photos to get signed. The more unusual the item—the far more likely a star would be to stop and sign.

My father, as an amateur photographer at the time, found he would garner a lot of business from players who would hire him to do shots for them. They would later pass these out to fans for them to hand back to the player to be signed. As was often the case, the player would end up having the shoot for free and only paying for materials. After all, Dad was a fan first also. So Dad always had the "good stuff" a player had never seen.

Getting ready for the next day's adventure meant that organization was rule number one for me. Everything alphabetized, paper clipped, and ready to pull out on a moment's notice. We would discuss what players might not be traveling with the team, and what player or Hall of Famers just might show up at this or that particular game. All Star games, Playoff games, and World Series were great for those. Something Oakland had a lot of in the early '70's.

It was always early to bed the night before and we would leave before the sun came up for the players' hotel. With

**Pete And Annette
Viewing The Results
Of A Good Day Out With Dad**

Sandlot Stories

materials in hand, and a pocket full of new sharpie pens, (ball points always caused problems on waxed cards and glossy photos), we were off to any number of particular hotels that the visiting teams would use.

Arriving at the hotel we would stand patiently, quietly, and well dressed, usually waiting somewhere near the coffee shop where they all headed early in the morning.

When Dad saw someone walking down the hall he would quietly whisper the name to me, in case I didn't recognize him on my own. Then my frantic scramble into my overfilled file would begin. As a youth I was always chasing behind Dad, just too slowly. Though it never once was a race, I just didn't have my "chops" down yet.

As I grew and developed my own autograph request style, I always felt Dad was proud to let me lead the way. I was polite, grateful, never pushy and had unique items of my own to have signed. It was obvious we were a team, but two who loved the sport and the players. It was barely anything called a hobby at the time. Just keep sakes of a special moment in time. We often found ourselves chatting with the players before breakfast. We even found ourselves having breakfast with them in later days when they would recognize us. There was no frantic hunt, not even another autograph seeker most of the time.

My first autograph I got was Spring Training 1962. I was three, and it was a young Willie Mays. I would like to say I remember it, but I was a little young to show the etiquette I was later taught in the fine art of autograph requests. I can only hope my diaper was clean and my hat on straight.

Sandlot Stories

Not all of my memories are wonderful, and blissful either. There was the time when I was about eleven years old, that too many paper clips got tangled in my file and I was slow to pull out my card. This was no "cup of coffee player" either, it happened to be Roberto Clemente. I received one royal tongue lashing from the star, making him wait and all. I guess I only get it from the best, and this one I never forgot. Nor did my father. In later years, he never let me forget that one. It was all tongue in cheek though. Sadly, I would never have another chance to right this with Mr. Clemente, as he would be killed in a plane crash a few short months later. All in all, it was a fantastic way to meet the players. They dressed like rock stars, had groupies, and were truly respectful and kind to the fan.

From the hotel we would travel over to the ballpark. The early birds had dined and left. The "late-nighters" might just miss breakfast and go directly to the park where we would hopefully catch them rushing in. Here we could also get the home team signatures, and have another chance at the visiting team bus.

That was always a total free-for-all; thirty players off in three minutes. If you got more than five or so autographs, you were doing well. It was a panic stricken few moments for me (post Clemente lashing), so I learned to pick and choose exactly who I was going to ask for a signature, gambling on the fact that they were even in the bus. Some out of town players might have family and friends in the area and not come in on the bus.

I am mostly speaking about the Oakland ballpark in the

Sandlot Stories

early 1970's. We had befriended a few of the guards, and they would let us stand in by the players' entrance gate. Usually that entire player lot was off limits. But the closer it came to game time, the more fans found their way over to the entrance. Charles Finley, owner of the A's, was one you really had to read from a distance. If he looked receiving, he would gladly sign something for you. But if he was busy, he would have that "walk—don't even consider it" look, or in fact, "step back a few steps and clear the path." It was always fun for me to see another fan not know this well learned lesson of mine.

One day Reggie Jackson pulled up in his 1940 Chevrolet coupé hotrod. There was a different car every day for Reggie. Being sixteen years old at the time, I was involved in restoring a 1940 sedan myself. As Reggie was signing something for me, I told him about my project at home. His response was, "Sure you are kid, sure you are." Oh well, those who have met Mr. October probably aren't too surprised to hear that one. I wasn't either. It was always fun to see what players drove. The new rookies had the expensive imports, the Hall of Famers had Cadillacs or just as easily an old unassuming car their mother might have willed them. Never any pattern, this was usually the last chance for autographs. From here, it was in for the game.

I said last chance for autographs, but that isn't exactly the case. It was last chance for me. I found the mad struggle at the top of the dugout for player signatures during batting practice too much to deal with. Instead, I would sit proudly a few feet away and watch practice while thumbing through

Sandlot Stories

my autographs of the morning.

I watched my hero down on the field in those days. He didn't have a bat or a glove, but three cameras slung around his neck and a photographer's field pass.

Play Ball!!!

— Pete Dobbins
Alamo, California

Sandlot Stories

Dick Dobbins

By A Step

"That's silly. We have a perfectly beautiful backyard and you want to carve the area into one half of a baseball infield?" My Dad looked rather sheepishly into my Mom's fiery black eyes and muttered, "It won't deface the back yard. It will give it some character."

Thus started the "Project" in mid March, 1944 in Spokane, Washington—fine tuning our backyard to create the exact dimension of the third base section of an infield. That's correct, the right side of the infield only, from the pitcher's mound over. Over at first base my Dad plugged a large six-foot pole and to the pole attached a matted laundry tub device, which acted as the target for a well-placed throw. Dad wanted me to play third base and he was going to the extreme to teach me this position.

The landscaping project carried us into and through April. Blisters and scraped knees were our badges from learning about leveling the playing field. At eight years old, the task was exciting and I was spending time with my father, which was gratifying since he was the best baseball player I knew.

May first we flicked a light on at the garage which was where the third base dugout would have been. Oh my gosh, the field, illuminated by the floodlight took on a magic all its own.

"Now the 'Repetition' begins." My father stated. Out came the Fungo bat (a longer bat than normal designed for infield

195

Sandlot Stories

practice), the bucket of balls (never did find out where he got them all) and a to-do list prepared by Dad that outlined what the "Repetition" consisted of (gulp!!). The practice consisted of ten minutes of stretching—my Dad was ahead of his time—and playing catch.

The script then called for fifty ground balls being hit to me from home plate. Yes, there was a regulation home plate buried about thirty feet from the backdoor. My Mom really loved that! I was stationed forty-five feet away from home plate, down the third base side and required to "take" ground balls and throw to the post and of course into the muffled tub at first base.

My baseball experience began that spring and summer along with the start of dreams and aspirations about playing baseball to the best of my ability. Fifty ground balls every morning prior to going to school meant getting up at 5:30 AM and being on the "Field" at six. In the summer, practice time stayed the same and more often than I wanted, "double days" became a term I detested. The summer faded and cool fall replaced the heat while the ritual and Repetition continued.

My start at forty-five feet gave way to fifty-five feet then sixty. The post stayed the same and surprisingly the thuds became a regular part of the noises associated with our backyard. There was the crack of the ball on the Fungo, the leather sound as I managed to field the ball, the silence as my feet properly took over, then the satisfactory sound as my first baseman received the throw; beating that imaginary runner by a step. How I loved that symphony of sounds!

Sandlot Stories

Then I'm nine, almost ten years old, back at ninety feet and squinting at that post. The large mouth of the tub had been replaced by a much smaller one, matted of course, but alarmingly tiny in its diameter. The practices continued and now I asked the question, "When can I go out and play with my friends?" Dad simply stated, "When I think you're ready."

The agony and the satisfaction that covered my years from eight until about ten were wonderful times between a father and son. But, it wasn't all good all the time. There were countless times when I took my position, almost in tears, because I didn't want to be there. Countless times when the weather would, I was certain, by my friend and cancel the practice. No chance! My father would stretch the warm ups and promise if I flawlessly executed my fielding and throwing, we would stop at only thirty-five ground balls.

Much to my surprise, I was acquiring that baseball rhythm expected of a player playing the "hot corner." I was acquiring a "good glove" and my arm was finding the mark at first. In my mind I was throwing the runner out by two strides. This was my birth as a potential ball player. But, the time, the love, the patience, the desire for me to be the best demonstrated by my father was not appreciated by this ten year old, until much later when like a bolt that mixture of patience, kindness, courtesy, and good temper exhibited by him was recognized.

Our neighborhood was almost entirely void of children my age. Three blocks away the baseball world I wanted to join existed. However, the playing age required by the players

Sandlot Stories

was at least twelve years old, preferably thirteen to fourteen. This was the sandlot rule, until then we had to watch.

The neighborhood team was good. The field was questionable compared to mine. There was no grass, and I swear the field seemed to lean upward toward home plate. The outfield was shallow, two hundred feet at best, because Lacy Street ran across it. There was no right field because the Concannon house rudely eliminated the need for one. A large telephone pole was situated in left center field and proved at times a hazard to the players. It was not much of a field to look at, but that's where the action was. Oh how I wanted the privilege of playing on that diamond.

Returning home after watching our neighborhood team win yet again and hearing them set up the next scheduled game for the championship; I felt left out and was grumbling about not being old enough. In other words, I was feeling very sorry for myself. I expressed this to my Dad and he just told me, "Your time will come. Let's go hit some grounders." "Doesn't he understand?" I said to myself. "I'm ready to play."

One Saturday morning, as my father was on his way out the door, he told me I had visitors. Outside our house were assembled the ball team I wanted to play for: Al, Greg, Ron, David, Kenny, Jimmy, Lee—eight! No, wait, seven!

Al, the spokesman, told me that the team was in dire need of a third baseman because Wendell was sick. He wanted to know if I could take his spot. (Gulp!) I glanced at my Dad getting into the car.

He nodded and mouthed to me, "You're ready."

Sandlot Stories

With a great deal of bravado, certainly more than I felt inside, I said, "You bet!"

Al advised me that game time was one and half hours away and the team we were playing would travel several blocks to, according to their spokesman, "Kick our butts!"

Wow, "The Sandlot Bigs!" I shouted into the mirror. What a break. Thanks, Wendell. Am I ready? "You bet!" I said. "You heard what your Dad said!"

The field's playing area still sloped uphill, the light pole was still in left center field, there was no need for a right fielder because the Concannon's house was still there. However, the magic spell that followed me to the field was real.

An umpire, standing behind the pitcher, had been acquired from some mid point between the neighborhoods to assure fairness. Infield practice was taking place...and then suddenly—it was game time!

The first pitch delivered, by Al, was promptly hit over our center-fielder's head and bounced into the back of a pick-up truck going North on Lacy Street. Some beginning! We played six full innings and were ahead by one as the visitors came to bat in the top of the seventh. My excitement and my jitters quickly disappeared about as fast as the ball in the back of that pick-up. I fielded several balls hit to me and made the throws to first.

"Routine." I say to myself.

However, I was reminded of a statement my father would constantly say to me during our infield drills. "Michael, please do not get an excessively high opinion of yourself." "Play within your capabilities and stay intense."

Sandlot Stories

I settled down and realized that we had two outs, they had a runner on second and the "big guy" was at the plate. Al was running on empty, so I took two more steps to the right, really recovering the line.

Then the countless ground balls, the demanding throw from third, the proper movement of the feet, all came to fruition as the hitter pulled a ball down the line saying, "Triple!" all the way. My reaction was timed right. I had the ball in my glove, made the pivot and yes, I threw the runner out, by a step! End of game! We win!

There were lots of pats on the backs from my playmates and some comments from the parents who had watched. But the best moments were on the walk home. I had nothing to say, I just walked the sweet walk of victory and realized that our sandlot ballpark was "my house." I had played with the guys and made a difference.

Then I realized that my Dad, who had never showed up, would have to hear play-by-play details of the entire game. I also realized then and there that those backyard drills—the "When you're ready" routine had put me in this position. What a team—my Dad and I! Then I wondered why he missed the game.

My Mom was sitting on the porch, waiting for me as I approached our home. Her eyes were very red and it looked like she had been doing a lot of crying. I thought perhaps she was crying because I had done so well in the game—tears of joy.

Then Mom told me that my father had been killed in an auto accident on his way home to the game.

Sandlot Stories

• • •

Years later, when I was a freshman in high school playing on a very good varsity baseball team, I bought my Dad a ticket right behind third base.

— *Mike*

Sandlot Stories

The Level Playing Field

Some of my favorite childhood memories go back to playing baseball in our backyard in Jonesboro, Arkansas when I was between the ages of six and nine. We were a Northern family coming into this southern town. My father, a minister, was born in Philadelphia, Mom hailed from Boston, my brother and I were born in Ohio, my sister in New York—we are clearly Northerners and it was the 1950's south. For us, everything seemed strange and new. I remember coming home from school one day and telling my mother that someone had told me to turn "Rat" soon figuring out that it meant to turn right. Just understanding people was a new experience for us, but then again they thought we spoke a strange language.

Even before we got to Arkansas I had begun my love affair with baseball. It probably had to do with a couple of things. One was the baseball game we used to go to in Kansas City when we lived in the projects and my dad was in Seminary. We would ride the bus for what seemed a very long time to sit in the "always cheap" seats for a family outing to see the Kansas City Athletics. I can remember falling asleep on my dad's shoulder on the bus ride home after a double header that must have ended long after my bedtime. The other had to do with television. We first got a TV in 1953. They started putting baseball games on early in black and white, and since it was one of the few shows available, we

Sandlot Stories

watched. So by the time we moved to Arkansas, baseball was just natural.

In past places that we had lived, the backyard was whatever you could create out of cinders, rocks, and a few weeds. But when we got to Arkansas, to the parsonage where we were to live, we found this wonderfully huge back yard—half of which was this miry, red clay. Certainly not a picturesque back yard, but for us as kids, it was perfect for setting up a baseball field. We found some old roof tiles and we made those into the bases. Then because we were prone to putting out the windows in the back of the house during games, Dad helped us cover the windows with plywood to protect them.

Because we were new in the neighborhood and because, even at that time, it was a small enough town, (I think it was about 25,000 people) we were considered outsiders. Especially since we were Northerners. When we moved there it was 1956 and in 1964 was the Civil Rights Movement. I had never entered a culture where lines were so clearly drawn. And in fact when we first got there, there was a lot of pushback. I remember when I first entered grade school—"Well you don't speak like us."— "Here's what we believe"— "Here's what we are thinking." It was constantly this pushback. As a kid you just want to fit in, but at the same time there is a part of you that says something is not right here.

But there is something about baseball that is the common ground that helped to get us started with the other kids. In the beginning, there was my brother, my older sister, myself, the kid next door, and with a kid two doors down we began

Sandlot Stories

to play baseball together almost every evening.

It began with this attraction of playing catch together in the backyard and than pretty soon we had enough for a small team and "everyone" could play. It didn't matter where they came from or who they were or that they were a Northerner or Southerner or what they believed in, it was just a great leveler.

I think about the fun that we had, it was every night—I mean when we were not practicing piano or doing homework we were out there in the backyard playing ball! We would play until you could not see anymore and it didn't matter if you got injured. I've still got a crooked small finger from not catching a fly ball in the sun. But I never see it as crooked, just a trophy and a reminder of wonderful fun!

We didn't have much in the way of equipment. We had a ball that was barely stuffed together with tape—it got wrapped and re-wrapped, because we couldn't afford a new softball. But we didn't care. It was just the shear joy of coming together and playing until we were exhausted, or the sun went down, or someone came to call us for supper. And as I look back on that now, I see God in that field.

It was the great leveler. He really created the sense of baseball for us. The idea of this active rest, active play, where we could just enjoy one another's company. I have incredibly fond memories of that time that dot the landscape of everything I have done since. For example, when I was nine years old I got my first bat and ball as a birthday gift—my very own! I never cared much for dolls…and I was absolutely thrilled to death to have my own bat and ball. The first thing I did was go out and share it with the neighborhood.

Now, like I said, it played a big part in my life and to this very day I still ask for this kind of gift, because I think it represents the chance to play together, to be a team, with everyone equal. I know that we try to talk about who's better at throwing or pitching or batting or things, but I really think it's about the fact that once you get going as a team there is this sense of extended family, which is really what God creates in our hearts. Since God wrote His love in our hearts, baseball is one of the ways He uses to help us define one another in that sense of God's family. Like I said, "suddenly" all differences melted away and it was just a bunch of kids and even sometimes my Dad would join us out there—just having a lot of fun! And nobody worried about what your cultural background was or where you came from or what you believed. It was just the ability to see one another on a level playing ground and like I said I think that was always God's intent. He provides those ways for us to see Him. Just like in the creation of the sunset and the sunrise. Why can't God be seen in the baseball game? In the togetherness and the fun of playing. It can! It begins in those little moments on the sandlot, when you know your family! You look around and it's a bunch of different people from all backgrounds and beliefs and it doesn't matter.

As I look back, I think that in this strangeness and alienation God provided this backyard. It was not a "gardener's paradise"—it had this red yucky clay, which was half the yard, and then there was grass which had been

Sandlot Stories

trampled on, and the other half was this huge area—it was a natural mud wall that went up to some woods in the back. To me it was great, it was a backstop, right! God clearly made that backyard to be a baseball field, because it wasn't good for much else! You could not raise a garden in it. And we thought that way. That backyard broke down a lot of barriers because once we got a handful of kids laughing and the rest of the neighborhood could hear the sounds, the other kids started coming—"Can we play?" "Can we play?" Frankly I don't remember as much about picking the sides as—"Yeah, get out there in centerfield." "Get over here!" It was just like "Come on—join the game!" It was always a game in progress and it was never finished and we never cared who won. It was just the sheer joy of playing. It was God's level playing field.

— Suzanne or "Suzie" in those days!

• • •

I loved #24 for the Giants' Willie Mays because he was the complete player and a classy guy with loads of enthusiasm for the game of baseball and life. And besides, he was a leveler!

"I Could" by Theresa Lacey
Incline Village, NV

This is a painting of the baseball field, Preston Field, in Incline Village, NV, showing a little player dreaming of what he/she could become.

It is dedicated to Theresa's brother,

Danny Kirkmeyer

who always wanted to play baseball and is now playing in Baseball Heaven.

Printed in the United States
1273900001B/1-66